11/5/09

11/18/16

5/13/18 (~~schim~~)
(SKIM)

4/24/19

8/17/19

Unmixing the Intellect

Recent Titles in
Contributions in Philosophy

UNMIXING THE INTELLECT

Aristotle on Cognitive Powers and Bodily Organs

Joseph M. Magee

Contributions in Philosophy, Number 86

GREENWOOD PRESS
Westport, Connecticut · London

Library of Congress Cataloging-in-Publication Data

Magee, Joseph M., 1965–
    Unmixing the intellect : Aristotle on the cognitive powers and bodily
organs / Joseph M. Magee.
        p. cm.—(Contributions in philosophy, ISSN 0084–926X ; no. 86)
    Includes bibliographical references and index.
    ISBN 0–313–32377–1 (alk. paper)
    1. Aristotle. De intellectu. 2. Intellect—History. 3. Mind and body—
History. 4. Senses and sensation—History. I. Title. II. Series.
    B415.A8M34   2003
    128'.2—dc21   2002069635

British Library Cataloguing in Publication Data is available.

Library of Congress Catalog Card Number: 2002069635
ISBN: 0–313–32377–1
ISSN: 0084–926X

First published in 2003

Greenwood Press, 88 Post Road West, Westport, CT 06881
An imprint of Greenwood Publishing Group, Inc.
www.greenwood.com

Printed in the United States of America

The paper used in this book complies with the
Permanent Paper Standard issued by the National
Information Standards Organization (Z39.48–1984).

10 9 8 7 6 5 4 3 2 1

Copyright Acknowledgments

The author and publisher gratefully acknowledge permission for the use of the
following material:

Joseph M. Magee, "Sense Organs and the Activity of Sensation in Aristotle,"
    Phronesis XLV, no. 4 (November 2000). Courtesy of Brill Academic
    Publishers.
Selections from *Essays on Aristotle's* De Anima, edited by Marsha S. Nussbaum
    and Amélie Oksenberg Rorty. Oxford: Clarendon Press, 1992. Reprinted by
    permission of Oxford University Press.

To Maria, for her love, support and patience.

Contents

Preface

This work began as an investigation into just one passage in Aristotle's *De Anima*: "It is necessary then that the mind, since it thinks all things, should be unmixed. . . . For the intrusion of anything foreign hinders and obstructs it." As I hope will become clear, there are several problems with this passage as it stands, not least of which is its translation. In the course of trying to make sense of these cryptic remarks of Aristotle, I was led to explore his views, not only on the mind, but also on sensation, and it was from there that I came into contact with those scholars who interpreted Aristotle in the light of contemporary philosophy of mind. What I came to discover is that Aristotle's views on the intellect do, in fact, form a coherent whole with his views on the senses, and that many of his contemporary interpreters are misled by modern theories and so misread his views on both the senses and the intellect. I hope that this book will disentangle Aristotle's theory of intellect from those of some of his modern interpreters.

I would like to thank the students and faculty of the Center for Thomistic Studies at the University of Saint Thomas, Houston, Texas. By taking Aristotle's doctrine seriously, they have helped me to make the issues involved at least clearer, and thereby to point me in what seems to be the right direction, on both interpretive and philosophical matters. I hope that the present book is of more than mere historical interest, for, as St. Thomas remarked in his own interpretation of Aristotle, philosophy is not concerned (only) with what others have thought, but seeks to know what is the truth of things. If the present work does not show what the truth of things is concerning the intellect, hopefully, it will at least indicate what Aristotle actually thought about the intellect.

Introduction

A philosopher's predispositions and preoccupations often condition his or her approach to the philosophical study of human beings. This is perhaps especially true of those who undertake an exposition of Aristotle's psychological theory as contained in his treatise *Περί Ψυχῆς* whose title is usually translated as *On the Soul*. As this title suggests, Aristotle makes significant use of some notion of soul, but this idea is laden with various supervening connotations that tend to color a philosopher's study of Aristotle's theory. The source of these connotations for contemporary interpreters of Aristotle has less to do with his own theory than with the distinct, yet related, history of the notion of soul.

The roots of this rich notion stretch back in Western thought long before Aristotle tried to give a coherent philosophical account of soul in the fourth century B.C. Yet, however important the notion of soul was for ancient Greek philosophy, it also proved to be of great religious importance, especially with the advent of Christianity. For Christians, soul has come to signify that by which individuals survive bodily death and become permanently united with God. It therefore assumes singular religious significance insofar as it is essentially endowed with immortality. Focusing on this religious significance, soul comes to be understood primarily in opposition to the body, as the whole or part of a human that, at death, exists separated from the body. Thus, a person's body may die, but his or her soul does not. Moreover, insofar as eternal life is open to human beings alone, soul is conceived not only as opposed to the body, but also as the exclusive possession of human beings.

René Descartes in the seventeenth century crystallized this dualistic opposition between body and soul in his own dualism of mind and matter. He identified the human person with mind and defined mind, at least in part, as being in opposition to matter. With consciousness as its defining characteristic, unextended mind (*res cogitans*) is so opposed to extended matter (*res extensa*) as to be incapable of directly interacting with it. Katherine Wilkes sketches the process by which the Cartesian mind supplanted soul, marveling at the rapidity with which the conscious *mens* supplants Aristotle's *psuche*.[1] Quoting the "Reply to the Fifth Set of Objections," Wilkes cites Descartes's desire to distinguish the principle for the activities shared with other animals from the principle of thought proper to humans. According to Descartes, "when soul is taken to mean *the primary actuality* or *chief essence of man*, it must be understood to apply only to the principle by which we think, and I have called it by the name *mind*."[2] The Christian tension between body and soul accordingly grew into a gulf between mind and matter, one which philosophers are still struggling to heal. Soul, as conscious mind, came to be seen, not simply in contrast to the body in the sense of being immune to bodily corruption, but as essentially opposed to and without any intrinsic relation to the body. Dualism was the nearly inevitable result after Descartes made consciousness the defining characteristic of an essentially non-extended mind, for it created a view of the mind where the inner consciousness mirrors the exterior material reality, but left unexplained how the mirroring could be accomplished.[3] Because of its essential opposition to the body, opponents of Descartes tend to view the soul as the source of the problems engendered by this opposition.

Thus, special interest, both positive and negative, comes to be placed on the human soul and the extent to which it exists in opposition to the body. If one's religious convictions require that the soul not be subject to corruption, one may approach the discussion of the soul in this vein. Similarly, owing to predispositions antagonistic to these religious views, or sensing the difficulties inherent in viewing the soul or its operations as opposed to the body (in reaction to Cartesian dualism), one may deny any activity or existence of the soul separate from the body. A theorist of the latter type would, perhaps, try to offer an account of human beings and their activities that has no recourse to a soul in basic opposition to the body. These attitudes are also found among interpreters of Aristotle.

Aristotle wrote the first attempt at a systematic account of perceptual and mental activity in his work titled *Περί Ψυχῆς* (sometimes given in Latin as *De Anima* and sometimes translated as *On the Soul*). Aristotle uses ψυχή as an explanatory device to account for all vital activity, not just conscious mental activity. Thus, the question of whether what Aristotle refers to as ψυχή is the same as what we refer to as "soul" naturally presents itself. As the principle of activities that involve the body (e.g., digestion), ψυχή clearly is not the same as Descartes's redefinition of soul as conscious mind. Seeing the sterility of Descartes's "mind," some interpreters emphasize the difference between Aristotle's ψυχή and the Cartesian-tainted notion of "soul." For some, it is precisely its difference from Descartes's that commends Aristotle's theory. Thus, there is renewed interest in Aristotle's *De Anima* (*DA*) and his other psychological treatises among contemporary philosophers. Aristotle, it is argued, has a theory of vital, sensitive and mental activity that does not commit its adherents to any sort of soul that is opposed to the body in the Cartesian sense.[4] Indeed Aristotle's conception of soul is defined in relation to the body (412a20–21), so that it is misguided to ask whether soul, as form of the body, could exist apart from the body (412b6–7). Aristotle is thus enlisted into the post-Cartesian debate about the solution to the mind-body problem on the side of those who deny that mind (or soul) is opposed to matter and the body. Accepting the reality of the material side of the mind-body dichotomy, many anti-dualists interpret Aristotle as a kind of materialist and his version of soul (i.e., ψυχή) as consistent with materialism. While few, if any, of his contemporary interpreters recommend reading Aristotle as reducing soul to the body, many believe that his doctrine embodies some sort of materialist theory of mind, either functionalist or, at least, a form of non-reductive materialism wherein mental states supervene on physical states.

A fly, however, appears in this Aristotelian salve for the wound left from dualism's separation of soul from body. Aristotle appears to claim at various points in the *De Anima*,[5] especially in Chapters 4 and 5 of Book 3, that part of the soul is immaterial in a sense that is too strong to allow for any materialist interpretation. He seems to say that a significant part of human activity—the part, in fact, that is distinctive of

human beings, that is, intelligent behavior—implies that the part of the
soul by which a person accomplishes that behavior is separate from the
body: "It is necessary then that mind, since it thinks all things, should
be unmixed" (429a18).[6] "So it is unreasonable to suppose that (the
mind) is mixed with the body" (429a24). Unlike other powers of the
soul, intellectual activity is not realized in any bodily organ (429a27).
Given these statements by Aristotle, *DA* 3.4 apparently is supposed to
show that the operation of intellect does *not* take place anywhere in the
body and, thus, that the intellect itself is an immaterial power. Aristotle,
then, appears not to be a thoroughgoing materialist when he considers
the intellect. Indeed, some functionalist interpreters concede that his
conception of νοῦς (i.e., mind or intellect) is an unfortunate embarrassment.[7] If Aristotle's position on the intellect is integral to his whole
account, however, then his theory is not easily assimilable to functionalism. Furthermore, if Aristotle's arguments succeed in showing the
strong immateriality of the intellect, then they also show the falsity of
materialism in general as a complete explanation of human beings.

There are those, however, who would enlist Aristotle into the materialist camp in the war between body and soul by maintaining that he
did not intend to claim that the intellect is separate. According to Michael Wedin, for example, Aristotle's assertions that νοῦς is unmixed
are offered merely as support for the contention that the mind is nothing
actual until it thinks.[8] Drawing on a cognitivist conception of mental
states, Wedin argues that receptive mind, while having no specific physical organ, nevertheless depends on a set of bodily structures, and is
realized in these bodily structures as a higher-level functional organization of the person. Thus, according to Wedin, mind as described in
DA 3.4 is not spatially separable, but separable only in thought (429a10).
Before evaluating the validity of any argument for the conclusion that
νοῦς is separate from the body, one must first consider Wedin's view
that Aristotle does not intend to prove this conclusion in *DA* 3.4.

Despite the misgivings of Wedin, Aristotle nevertheless seems to offer
three arguments that νοῦς is a non-bodily power. In the conclusions of
these arguments, he describes it as unmixed (429a18, 24) or as separate
from the body (429b6, 22). In all of the arguments, he seems to justify
his conclusions by at once asserting that νοῦς and sense are similar in
their cognitive activity, and yet that the activity of the senses has certain
characteristic features on account of their organs. Since νοῦς does not

have these characteristics, Aristotle concludes that it is not a power whose activity is realized in any bodily organ. In the first argument, Aristotle states that, presumably because the bodily organs in which sensation occurs restrict the range of objects of the senses, the fact that νοῦς can know all things implies that it is unmixed with the body (429a18–22). Second, the senses are dazzled by the intensity of their object because the intensity upsets the sense organ. However, because νοῦς is not so dazzled, Aristotle concludes that it is separate (429b1–6). Finally, the senses know material things composed of the elements because their organs are likewise so composed. Since essences are not the same as the things themselves, and since νοῦς knows the essence of things, νοῦς is separate from matter (429b11–22).

Despite the brevity of the summaries of these arguments, one can see that in all the arguments of *DA* 3.4 Aristotle bases his conclusions on a comparison between sense and intellect. The requirements of the arguments of this chapter indicate what the nature of this analogy is. In order to prove his conclusions, Aristotle needs to compare νοῦς and the sensitive faculty according to some feature that they share in common as cognitive powers. Moreover, this feature needs to involve bodily organs for the sense faculty so that when Aristotle specifies the differences between sensation and intellection according to this feature, he can show that the activity of νοῦς does not likewise involve bodily organs. For, if it were supposed that νοῦς was similar to the sensitive faculty, but in ways that for the senses did not somehow involve their organs, the differences between νοῦς and sense would not be relevant for showing that νοῦς has no organ.

Accordingly, Aristotle introduces *DA* 3.4 with a comparison between intellection and sensation according to what seems to be at least one point of comparison relevant for demonstrating that νοῦς is separate. He claims that the intellect is like the sense faculty in being receptive of form, and although he introduces this analogy as conditional, he presumably accepts it without argument (429a13–17). If the reception of form is a relevant point of comparison, then it needs to apply to νοῦς as well as to the sense faculty. For, unless the reception of form applies to both νοῦς and the senses, Aristotle would have no basis on which to conclude that νοῦς acts without the body.[9] So, in order to accept the conclusions Aristotle claims to demonstrate about the intellect, one apparently must first accept this view of what he means by the reception of form.

Just this point, however, has recently been seriously challenged. According to Richard Sorabji, Aristotle is speaking only of a physiological change in the sense organ when he claims that sensation is the reception of form without matter.[10] Sorabji distinguishes himself from another group of interpreters, which includes Aquinas and most of the ancient commentators,[11] who believe that the reception of form without matter describes the act of the sense faculty becoming aware of its objects. Thus, the evaluation of *DA* 3.4 depends upon first evaluating these claims of Sorabji. For, if Sorabji is right and νοῦς is not like the sense faculties in being receptive of form, even though such receptivity may bear some relationship to having an organ, nevertheless, the activity of νοῦς will imply nothing about whether νοῦς has an organ. In evaluating Sorabji's interpretation, it should become clear whether or not he is accurate in his assessment of Aquinas as well.

Next, supposing it can be shown that νοῦς is like sense in the relevant ways, one must understand what effect having an organ has for the sensitive faculty. Since Aristotle compares the two powers in order to draw conclusions from their apparent differences, one must understand as much as possible about each term of the comparison. For instance, it seems that it is in virtue of the fact that the senses have organs that undergo some kind of physical change that Aristotle sometimes says that sensation is a kind of being affected (416b33–35).[12] Yet he also says that if sense is a sort of being acted upon and a kind of alteration, it is a special sort that should receive a special name (417a22–b22). Furthermore, he says that sense, like νοῦς is impassive (429a15), but that the impassivity of each is not the same (429a30). Stephen Everson has offered an interpretation of Aristotle's perceptual theory wherein the activity of perceptual awareness supervenes on the physical and literal assimilation of sense organs to their objects.[13] Thus, the awareness of a red object comes about when, and because, an eye has become literally as red as the object seen. In evaluating these claims of Everson's, it will become clear to what extent sensation is either an alteration or an activity (or both), to what extent this occurs in the physical constitution of sense organs, and what implications these facts have for sense cognition. Thus, the affectation of the sense organ, or the sense power in its organ, seems to imply certain things about the capacity of the senses. Finding a consistent interpretation of Aristotle's theory, while difficult, is necessary for a full understanding of his distinction between sense and νοῦς.

Finally, one must consider what specifically the characteristics are that Aristotle says distinguish νοῦς from sense and differentiate it to the point that he can conclude that νοῦς has no organ. If, for instance, Aristotle claims that νοῦς knows all things, one must understand why this fact would imply that it is unmixed, that it is separate in some strong sense. Again, one must try to discover why the failure of intensely intelligible objects to dazzle νοῦς entails that it is separate. Finally, one must see whether he can justify his conclusion that, because the essences of some things are not the same as the things themselves, the power that grasps essences is separate. If Aristotle can establish the truth of these claims, given the truth of the claims that preceded them, he will have shown that νοῦς is unmixed and separate from the body.

The foregoing considerations should indicate with sufficient clarity the order and content of this book. In the first chapter, I survey the major contemporary philosophical positions on the relation between mind and body, laying emphasis on the implications of materialist theories and their use in the development of interpretations of Aristotle's doctrines of sense and mind. Next, in Chapter 2, I argue that *DA* 3.4 was written to demonstrate that the intellect is spatially separate, and that the claims of Michael Wedin cannot stand against the overwhelming textual evidence throughout the *DA* supporting this conclusion. Supposing that Aristotle sought to demonstrate the separateness of the intellect, in Chapter 3 I argue that Aristotle intended to claim that the intellect is like the sense faculty in being receptive of forms, against the interpretation of Richard Sorabji. In Chapter 4, I examine Aristotle's treatment of the senses in the light of Stephen Everson's interpretation that the act of perception supervenes on material alterations. I conclude that supervenience is incompatible with Aristotle's account of sensation, but that, for Aristotle, the fact that the senses have organs entails certain limitations for these cognitive powers. Finally, in Chapter 5, I offer an explanation and interpretation of Aristotle's doctrine of νοῦς in *DA* 3.4 and defend it against various alternate readings of, and objections to, Aristotle's arguments.

NOTES

1. K. V. Wilkes, "*Psuchē* versus the Mind," in *Essays on Aristotle's* De Anima, ed. Martha C. Nussbaum and Amélie Oksenberg Rorty (Oxford: Clarendon Press, 1992), pp. 109–128.

2. Ibid., p. 115. Cf. René Descartes, *The Philosophical Works of Descartes*, ed. and trans. E. S. Haldane and G.R.T. Ross, vol. 2 (Cambridge: Cambridge University Press, 1967), p. 210.

3. Wilkes, "*Psuchē* versus the Mind," p. 116.

4. Charles H. Kahn, "Aristotle on Thinking," in *Essays, on Aristotle's* De Anima, ed. Martha C. Nussbaum and Amélie Oksenberg Rorty (Oxford: Clarendon Press, 1992), pp. 359–380.

5. Hereafter refered to as *DA*.

6. Aristotle, *De Anima*, ed. W. D. Ross (Oxford: Clarendon Press, 1956). Unless otherwise noted, all citations of the *De Anima* will be from this edition.

7. K. V. Wilkes, *Physicalism* (Atlanta Highlands, NJ: Humanities Press, 1978).

8. Michael V. Wedin, "Tracking Aristotle's Νους", in *Aristotle*: De Anima *in Focus*, ed. Michael Durrant (New York: Routledge, Inc., 1993), pp. 128–161.

9. See Jonathan Lear, *Aristotle: The Desire to Understand* (Cambridge: Cambridge University Press, 1988), pp. 114–115.

10. Richard Sorabji, "Body and Soul in Aristotle," in *Aristotle*: De Anima in Focus, ed. Michael Durrant (New York: Routledge, Inc., 1993), pp. 162–196; see also idem, "Intentionality and Physiological Processes: Aristotle's Theory of Sense Perception," in *Essays on Aristotle's* De Anima, ed. Martha C. Nussbaum and Amélie Oksenberg Rorty (Oxford: Clarendon Press, 1992), pp. 195–227.

11. Richard Sorabji, "From Aristotle to Brentano: The Development of the Concept of Intentionality," in *Festschrift for A. C. Lloyd: On the Aristotelian Tradition*, ed. H. Blumenthal and H. Robinson, *Oxford Studies in Ancient Philosophy*, supp. vol. (Oxford: Oxford University Press, 1991).

12. "So in the case of sensation, since sensation in active operation is a change of state, this must also happen. Consequently this affection persists in the sense organs, both deep down and on the surface, not only while they are perceiving but also when they have ceased to do so" (*De Somno* 2, 459b4–7); see also Aristotle, *Aristotle's De Motu Animalium*, ed. Martha C. Nussbaum (Princeton: Princeton University Press, 1978), 701b15–25.

13. Stephen Everson, *Aristotle on Perception* (Oxford: Clarendon Press, 1997).

Abbreviations for Works of Aristotle

APo	*Posterior Analytics*
APr	*Prior Analytics*
DA	*De Anima*
De Caelo	*On the Heavens*
De Sensu	*On Sense and the Sensible Object*
De Somno	*On Sleep and Waking*
GC	*On Generation and Corruption*
Gen An	*On the Generation of Animals*
Ins	*On Dreams*
Mem	*On Memory and Recollection*
Meta	*Metaphysics*
Meteor	*Meteorology*
NE	*Nicomachean Ethics*
PA	*Parts of Animals*
Phys	*Physics*
Top	*Topics*

CHAPTER 1

Aristotle and Contemporary Theories of Mind

INTRODUCTION

In order to evaluate the various interpretations of Aristotle's theory of mind that are the focus of this book, it is necessary to get an overview of the contemporary theories of mind that influence and shape these interpretations of Aristotle. The interpretations that will occupy most of our attention are those of materialists. They are, in their various ways, inspired by reactions against dualist theories of mind, most notably the dualism of René Descartes. As will be clear, because of the problems in maintaining Descartes's distinction between mind and matter, many theorists after Descartes begin with the assumption that all reality is exclusively material, that is, that there are no nonmaterial entities or properties. They then seek in their various ways to present a coherent account of what mentality consists in, that is, what it is about the material things that exhibit signs of mentality in virtue of which they have minds. In the first place, some materialists seek to reduce mental phenomena to the action of certain material parts, in particular, the brain and central nervous system, of mentally endowed creatures. Next, seeing certain difficulties in a reductionist account of mind, other theorists propose that mind consists in the function performed by certain specifiable states of the organism. Finally, some theorists, again in reaction to their predecessors, return to a sort of dualism with regard to properties. Such theorists claim that mental properties supervene on physical properties but maintain that the explanatory priority lies with the material side of the dualism. While this chapter will examine each of these contemporary theories of mind, it is first necessary, since the contemporary theories are ultimately reactions against Descartes, to outline in more detail the features of Cartesian dualism and the difficulties it engenders.

CARTESIAN DUALISM

In his efforts to renew and reform the study of philosophy and establish it on firm footing, René Descartes, in his *Meditations Concerning First Philosophy*, recounts his program of methodic doubt whereby he was able to secure for himself the certainty of his knowledge. In the course of this enterprise, Descartes discovers that the fact of his doubting is itself undoubtable. He concludes that his own existence is likewise undoubtable since the act of doubting implies a subject engaged in it. "Thus, after having thought well on this matter, and after examining all things with care, I must finally conclude and maintain that this proposition: *I am, I exist*, is necessarily true every time that I pronounce it or conceive it in my mind."[1] After establishing to his own satisfaction the indubitability of his own existence, Descartes next considers what the nature of this thinking subject is, and in so doing, he initiates the great fissure between mind and body that philosophy has sought to bridge ever since. Since one can conceive of oneself thinking in the absence of any body as well as of any body without consciousness, and since for Descartes whatever attribute one can conceive an entity as lacking is not essential to it, he believes that thought does not belong to anything material, that is, any body. He cannot, however, conceive of himself as not thinking; he concludes, therefore, that "thought is an attribute which belongs to me; it alone is inseparable from my nature."[2] For Descartes, the distinguishing characteristic of mind, then, is the possession of consciousness.

From the very fact that I know with certainty that I exist, and that I find that absolutely nothing else belongs necessarily to my nature or essence except that I am a thinking being, I readily conclude that my essence consists solely in being a body which thinks or a substance whose whole essence or nature is only to think. And although perhaps, or rather certainly, as I will soon show, I have a body with which I am very closely united, nevertheless, since on the one hand I have a clear and distinct idea of myself in so far as I am only a thinking and not an extended being, and since on the other hand I have a distinct idea of body in so far as it is only an extended being which does not think, it is certain that this "I"—that is to say, my soul, by virtue of which I am what I am—is entirely and truly distinct from my body and that it can be or exist without it.[3]

As the sole possessor of consciousness, mind is completely opposed to matter, that is, it is unextended and so nonphysical. Matter, on the other hand, is completely devoid of thought, but is characterized by extension in which its physicality and spatiality consist. There are, then, two completely separate realms of reality for Descartes, mind and matter, and each has no characteristic in common with the other. Although Descartes believes that in human beings the two kinds of substances form a union, he has defined each such that it is difficult to understand how they can be united in a human person.

Unlike Descartes, Aristotle's commitment to embodied souls precludes the possibility that he is a strong dualist. Clearly for Aristotle, some of the mental states Descartes calls "thoughts" have a strong connection with the bodies of the animals to which they occur. "It seems that these affections of the soul are associated with the body—anger, gentleness, fear, pity, courage and joy, as well as loving and hating; for when they appear the body is also affected" (403a18–19). Indeed, the soul, in virtue of which an animal enjoys mental states in Aristotle's view, is a reality that must exist in a body: "one need no more ask whether body and soul are one than whether the wax and the impression it receives are one, or in general whether the matter of each thing is the same as that of which it is the matter" (412b6–7). The Aristotelian doctrine of soul, then, is clearly incompatible with the Cartesian mind.

In addition to the difficulties involved in interpreting Aristotle as consistent with the Cartesian theory of mind, it seems that the sort of dualism for which Descartes argues entails some insuperable problems of its own. It seems to be a characteristic of some of the things that he calls thoughts, for example, volitions, that they cause a material thing, for example, a person's arm, to move. Likewise, it seems that some material things, for example, yellow flowers, have the ability to cause a person to have thoughts, for example, sensations of yellow and beliefs about flowers. If minds are as distinct from material things as Descartes claims, it seems at least paradoxical that the two sorts of substances should interact. For, it seems beyond the scope of any coherent theory to explain how a completely nonphysical, nonspatial substance could exert causal influence on, and be causally affected by, physical bodies obeying necessary laws.[4] Because of the problems of reconciling material bodies with immaterial minds, the Cartesian dichotomy is usually simply rejected.

The idea that there are nonphysical substances outside the framework of spacetime and in causal interaction with physical processes, as Descartes believed, has seemed to many thinkers as deeply puzzling, mysterious, and ultimately incoherent. Thus, ontological physicalism, the view that there are no concrete existents, or substances, in the spacetime world other than material particles and their aggregates, has been a dominant position on the mind-body problem. In most contemporary debates, ontological physicalism forms the starting point of discussion rather than a conclusion that needs to be established.[5]

Since Cartesian minds entail more theoretical troubles than their explanatory power is worth, most contemporary thinkers begin their discussion with the other half of Descartes's dualism, that is, matter.

REDUCTIVE MATERIALISM

Opposition to Cartesian dualism, especially since the theoretical triumph of atomic theory, has usually taken the form of reductive materialism. According to this theory, the macroscopic properties of a physical object are reducible to the microstructure of, and interaction between, the object's atomic and molecular parts—that is, reductive materialism claims to explain fully the macroscopic features of things in terms of their microstructures by asserting that the two sorts of properties are strictly identical. "When X is identical to Y in the strict sense, we have one thing, not two. Socrates is identical to Xanthippe's husband. What we have two of here are names, 'Socrates' and 'Xanthippe's husband.' These names happen to pick out, or refer to, one and the same person."[6] Likewise, the macroscopic properties are explained by the microstructure in the sense that the two are claimed to be really the same, with the microstructure providing the more precise and basic description. Thus, the macroscopic features are always and only features of the material constituents arranged in a particular manner because, ultimately, they are just properties of the material constituents.

When this theory is applied to living things, an organism's vital functions, including the psychological and mental states of animals and humans, are believed to be reducible to the material elements that together constitute all there is to these organisms. "Mental states *are* physical states of the brain. That is, each type of mental state or process is *numerically identical with* (is one and the same as) some type of physical state or process within the brain or central nervous system."[7] Since mental states are merely brain states at a different, and less precise, level of description, eventually laws will be found whereby one can correlate neurophysiology with the mental states of conscious beings. "[M]ind-brain identities, it is claimed, are like 'theoretical identities' in the sciences like the following: Water is H_2O; heat is molecular motion; the cause of AIDS is infection by HIV; light is electromagnetic radiation."[8] Thus, for the reductive materialist, mental properties do not belong to immaterial minds in some mysterious interaction with the physical world. Mental properties are reduced to the physical properties of whatever has a mind; the mental property ultimately just turns out to be the result of the fundamental physical properties of some material things.[9] This view is undaunted by the observation that mental states have an introspectible, phenomenal character. For example, a pain (a favorite example of a mental state) has the characteristic of feeling sharp or dull, throbbing or aching, to oneself. The reductive materialist believes that this phenomenal character is theoretically explainable in terms of the microstructure of the brain in the same way that other macroscopic properties, like the rigidity of glass, can be explained by the microstructure of the material things that have these properties. "There would therefore be nothing particularly surprising about a reduction of our familiar introspectible mental states to physical states of the brain."[10] Even though neuroscience does not now have a precise enough understanding of the brain and central nervous system to actually provide such correlating laws, reductive materialists are confident they will be found.

Apart from any merits or deficiencies that this sort of materialism has as a complete explanation of living things, such a position is clearly at such variance with Aristotle's text as to be untenable as a valid interpretation of his thought. Aristotle believes that a satisfactory account of any substance, especially any living thing, must do more than merely list the material constituents of the thing. Taking "soul" to stand for whatever is the cause of movement in animals, Aristotle believes that none of the material constituents, or any set of constituents, can solely and of itself be the soul (406b16–26). Even to claim that it is not the parts alone but the arrangement of these parts that explains an organism's vital activity is not a sufficient account. For Aristotle, this view is equivalent to saying that the principle of movement and activity, that is, the soul, is a "harmony." For instance, in *DA* 1.4 Aristotle reports: "It is said that the soul is a harmony of some kind; for, they argue, a harmony is a blend or composition of contraries, and the body is composed of contraries" (407b30–32). Thus, according to the view "approved by the verdict of public opinion" (407b29) in Aristotle's day, as in ours, it is the harmonious composition of the various elements and compounds that make up the body that accounts for the life of the body. Aristotle, for various reasons, also rejects this sort of reduction as a sufficient explanation (407b32–408a30). Reductive materialism is another more sophisticated version of the ancient harmony theory, for both assert that a given mental state (or the soul as the principle of such states) results from and, in fact, is identical to the material thing's constitution from more basic material elements.[11] Since Aristotle clearly rejects the harmony theory, he thereby would reject reductive materialism.

The lack of fit between Aristotle's theory and reductive materialism is also seen as a point for commending Aristotle. According to Charles Kahn, Aristotle's philosophy of mental abilities is not merely a possible alternative to dualism or its denial in reductive materialism, but is necessary to avoid what he considers the futility of the last three centuries of philosophical conflict.[12] According to Kahn, the simple anti-dualist position of reductive materialism is just as untenable as Cartesian dualism for philosophical reasons, and since Aristotle is not a reductive materialist, he is free of one fruitless solution to mind-body opposition.

FUNCTIONALISM

Since reductive materialism will not work as an interpretation of Aristotle, some anti-dualist Aristotelians interpret his psychological theory as an ancient precursor to another contemporary materialist theory of mind, that of functionalism.

Functionalism is the theory that mental states are defined in terms of their relations to causal inputs, behavioral outputs, and other mental states. It holds that the same mental state may be *realized* by several different physical states or processes. Mental states cannot, therefore, be reduced to physical states. They are, rather, functional states of the physical systems that realize them.[13]

Strict reductionism maintains that the mental components can be reduced to, that is, identified with, the material components of whatever has the mental state. Thus, a given mental state would be strictly identified with a given physical state of the thing that has the mental state. For instance, it is often alleged that pain is (strictly to be identified with) the firing of C-fibers in the creature's brain; one is in pain if, and only if, one's C-fibers are firing. If one does not have C-fibers, or they are not firing, then one would not be in pain. This kind of strict identity has generally been discredited on empirical grounds—it does not appear that there is any one identifiable type of physical state that always and only accompanies every mental event of a given type (pains are not always and only C-fiber firings). Moreover, many animals that are significantly different in their neurological anatomy seem to have mental states that correspond to human ones.

Since it seems very plausible (if not actually the case with nonhuman animals) that these mental states can be instantiated in a variety of physical systems, functionalists do not identify a mental state with its physical realization, but with the function that a given physical state plays in the life of the organism. Thus, what is the mental state of pain for a human, composed of carbon and water, might have a very different physical instantiation from the same state in some other kind of animal or creature (e.g., an extraterrestrial made of crystalline compounds, or even a computer made of silicon). "That state, considered from a purely physical point of view, would have a very different make up from a human pain state, but it could nevertheless be identical to a human pain state from a purely functional point of view."[14] According to functionalists, since the lion, the extraterrestrial and the computer can all experience the mental state identical to human pain, that mental state cannot be strictly identified with various material properties specific to the things that have that state.

Functionalism is still a materialist position because it states that there is nothing other than material substances that accounts for mental phenomena. However, the mere material constituents, atoms and molecules, alone do not explain the conscious behavior. Rather, it is the arrangement or configuration of whatever constituents make up the conscious thing, that is, the functional arrangement of the parts, that explains the behavior. This arrangement, however, is not itself a substance, and conscious behavior is not, strictly speaking, a property of the material parts, since mentality is not claimed to belong exclusively to this kind of matter and no other.[15] Instead, functionalists believe that this functional organization could possibly be realized in many different sorts of matter. "What is important for mentality is not the matter of which the creature is made, but the structure of the internal activities which that matter sustains."[16] Mentality would be a feature of whatever has the appropriate functional organization, no matter what it is made of.

Functionalists, then, assert an overall materialist position, but deny the strict identification of mental states with physical states, which reductionism asserts. Functionalists claim that there is no more to a creature that manifests mentality than its material constituents; mentality is not a property unique to nonmaterial (Cartesian) minds. Nevertheless, mentality cannot be identified with the physical states of these thoroughly physical creatures in the way that reductive materialism claims they are. Functionalists, like behaviorists from earlier in this century, seek to explain mentality in terms of observable behavior, but they realize that mental states also have an irreplaceable reference to other mental states. Thus, pain is described as that state that results from physical injury to an organism, is likely to produce avoidance behavior in that organism given other mental states, for example, that it does not want to endure the pain for some reason more than it wants to avoid it, and believes such behavior will lead to the cessation of the pain, and so forth. A pain-state may also cause other mental states, for example, the desire for revenge, that may, in turn, lead to observable behavior.

Functionalism thus defines mental states in terms of the causal roles they play as resulting from stimuli or other mental states (or both), and as causing other mental states or behavior (or both). Accordingly, a mental state is characterized as the total physical organism functioning, or being inclined to function, in a certain way, that is, as having a certain disposition to produce the appropriate behavior and have associated mental states. It is therefore immaterial for providing an adequate explanation of a given mental state to inquire what a creature is made of.

Mental states are the internal physical states of an organism that bear a causal relation to stimuli (inputs), other mental states and behavior (outputs). Whatever instantiates the internal states that have these relations would be a subject of mental states, and the internal states that had these relations would be, by definition, mental states. "[A] given functional organization . . . is capable of being 'built into' structures of many different logically possible physical (or even metaphysical) constitutions."[17] According to functionalism, anything that is the subject of mental predicates must have its structures arranged in an appropriate functional organization; both physical and, it is claimed, spiritual (metaphysical) beings, if they have mental states, would have to fall under this description. "In characterizing mental states as essentially functional states, functionalism places the concerns of psychology at a level that abstracts from the teeming detail of the brain's neurophysiological (or crystallographic, or microelectronic) structure."[18] Thus, it is seen as a great advance over reductive materialism that mental states, according to the functionalist description, be multiply realizable, that is, compositionally plastic. Functionalism is believed to have greater explanatory power in that it claims that mental states can be realized in anything as long as the realization of the states has the defining relation to input, other states and outputs.

Although the functionalist account of mental states allows that they be compositionally plastic, that is, that they can, in theory, be realized in a variety of physical systems, such systems will still have certain similarities. Specifically, in order for any two systems to serve as realizations of the same mental states, they must be functionally isomorphic; they must each instantiate the same set of functional relations. "Two systems are functionally isomorphic if *there is a correspondence between the states of one and the states of the other that preserves functional relations.*"[19] Thus, it is in virtue of the functional relations between physical states of a system that it possesses mental states, that is, in order to have such states as defined by functionalism, its physical states must be related to each other in functionally specified ways. These functional relations are specified in a psychological theory such that whatever can be described by a psychological theory can also be said to have a certain functional organization.[20] Thus, functional relations are the causal relations between stimuli, other mental states and behavior as specified by a theory. It is just the nature of such a theory, so understood, to specify how certain psychologically significant events and states cause and are caused by other psychologically significant events and states. An entity has mental states only on the condition that its internal physical states instantiate functional relations, that is, the causal relations that a psychological theory postulates to exist between mental states.

For example, it is not necessary that a creature have C-fibers in its brain in order to be in pain, nor even that it have a brain, as we understand the term. If there were Martians whose anatomy and physiology were in no way similar to our own, but who had states that resulted from physical damage, and caused characteristic painlike behavior and other associated internal states, they would fulfill the functionalist definition for being in pain. Thus, Martians would have pain, even though they were not in the same physical state as a pained human. They would have pain because the totality of the organism would have the same (or sufficiently similar) functional organization as ourselves in virtue of which we have pains. As such, they and we would be functionally isomorphic. Insofar as identity theory entails a denial that creatures materially different from ourselves could have the same mental states, functionalists reason that identity theory is false. Thus even something as alien as a Martian, if it were functionally isomorphic to humans in its psychology, could be said to truly have pains even though it had different sorts of C-fibers.[21] The same holds for objects we do not normally consider to have mental states, for example, electronic computers. But, if a computer or a robot had states that served the same function as our mental states, it would have those mental states.

Functionalists, then, offer an explanation of mental life in terms of a psychological theory without claiming that mental states are identical to the physical properties of a system. Furthermore, they seek to specify the functional isomorphism abstractly by reformulating a psychological theory with the mental terms systematically replaced by variables. The relations between the variables preserve the relations that the theory asserts to hold between mental terms: "Let T be a psychological theory (of either common sense or scientific psychology) that tells us (among other things) the relations among pains, other mental states, sensory inputs, and behavioral outputs. Reformulate T so that it is a single conjunctive sentence with all mental state terms as singular terms; for example 'is angry' becomes 'has anger.'"[22] When T is rewritten with all the mental states explicitly enumerated, each mental state term can be replaced by a variable, and the reformulation will state abstractly that each mental state is what it is as T specifies the relations of each state to the others. Being in pain can then be defined abstractly: a given individual has pain if and only if he or she is in that state that is specified as pain by T in virtue of its relation to the other mental states, and he or she is the sort of thing to which T applies. "That is, one has pain just in case he has a state that has certain relations to other states that have certain relations to one another (and to inputs and outputs . . .)."[23] Pain is the abstract state that bears to the other terms specified by the theory (T) just the causal relation that the theory specifies. This sort of abstract formulation, then, allows functionalists to specify in non-mental terms the functional relations that need to obtain between states of a system in order for that system to have mental states. Significantly, it also frees functionalism from specifying the physical makeup of such a system.

If there is a theory for mental states (e.g., pain is the mental state caused by tissue damage and is inclined to produce the desire to flee, etc.), then one can describe that theory abstractly and define a mental state without recourse to other specifically mental properties, inputs or behavior. The mental state is instead defined in terms of the abstract causal relations that obtain between a given configuration of a system's parts and other configurations. Pain, then, may be defined as the property of a system that arises from certain environmental conditions of the system and causes other properties and behavior. "Pain is identified with an abstract causal property tied to the real world only via its relations, direct and indirect, to inputs and outputs."[24] Any system that had an internal state with these relations to other internal states would be in pain, according to functionalism. Something is in a state of pain, not by virtue of any of its physical properties, but by virtue of the causal role of that internal state.[25] The internal states are not explained as properties unique to human C-fibers, for example, or in mentalistic terms, but abstractly, as variables of the abstract formulation of a psychological theory.

Thus, functionalism is neither reductionistic in its definition of mental terms, nor are its definitions circular by referring only to other mental states. According to functionalism, a given system has a mind if and only if there are certain unspecified properties of that system (call them "states")[26] such that whatever causal relations that a psychological theory specifies to obtain between the mental entities (having a pain, believing

p) also obtain between the states. Any system whose internal states bear to one another the same causal relations that the psychological theory specifies is susceptible to the same psychological description according to the theory. Such systems, then, are functionally isomorphic. If a human, lion, Martian or computer acts, reacts and has internal states in a causal economy consistent with what a psychological theory postulates as being in pain, then the human, lion, Martian or computer is in pain.

Although not so reductivist as to assert a strict identity between the mental properties of an organism and the physical properties of its constituents, functionalism does claim that a system has states with certain causal roles only in virtue of the matter of which the system is made. While such causal roles may not be unique to the constituents of which a given system is made, nevertheless, such causal roles of the states result from these constituents. For this reason, Putnam says that a functional organization may be "'built into' structures of many different logically possible physical (or even metaphysical) constitutions." What is necessary for a system to have a mind according to the functionalist description is that it be composed of parts such that the parts constitute states of the system, and the parts in a given state cause other states. Even when functionalists claim that a nonphysical (metaphysical or spiritual) system could instantiate a certain functional organization, they conceive of such nonphysical systems as being made of parts in a certain configuration that cause other states to be realized.

Indeed, there seems to be no barrier to the functionalist materialist's asserting that any particular actual world mental event, state, or process could be—in some other possible world—non-physically realized. All one need do is invoke a possible world in which the systematic replacement of parts of the central nervous system involves their replacement by non-physical causal factors with the capacity to influence the other parts of the central nervous system in a way that exactly simulates the function of the replaced part (which we can imagine becomes deactivated).[27]

Thus, the causal role that a given state plays within an overall functional organization is understood to be due to the causal capacity of the parts (physical or metaphysical) of which a system is composed. Other matter (or bits of spirit) in the proper configuration may play the same causal role that, for example, the gray matter in a human brain plays. Accordingly, a human mind and all the corresponding mental states may be multiply realized in other sorts of material creatures or in spiritual creatures. "[A]s functional state identity theorists have often pointed out, a *non*physical state could conceivably have a causal role typical of mental state. In functional specification terms, there might be a creature in which pain is a functionally specified *soul* state."[28] However, the states of whatever system that have the theoretically specified causal roles do so because of the properties belonging to that system's constituents. Functionalism, then, is a sort of reductionism insofar as it claims that mental states are due to the functionally or causally relevant properties of an organism's material constituents, but that such properties may be had by the constituents of more than one type of organism.

So strong is the functionalists' commitment that functional organization is multiply realizable that they hypothetically broaden its extension to include nonphysical (i.e., metaphysical) realizations. Putnam's statement above gives evidence of this confidence. Nor has this commitment seemed to wane even as Putnam, in his 1988 *Representation and Reality*, has denied the theory's ability to completely explain the nature of mental states. Recently, in explaining the problems he sees as insurmountable for functionalism, Putnam relates the following:

My "functionalism" insisted that, in principle, a machine (say one of Isaac Asimov's wonderful robots), a human being, a creature with silicon chemistry, and, if there be disembodied spirits, a disembodied spirit could all work much the same way when described at the relevant level of abstraction, and it is just wrong to think that the essence of our mind is our "hardware." This much—and it was central to my former view—I do not give up in my new book (*Representation and Reality*), and indeed it still seems to me to be as true and as important as it ever did.[29]

The functionalist description of the mind is thus seen to be truly universal, applying not only to physical creatures that have mental states, but also to spiritual creatures.

Their claim that even nonphysical entities (disembodied spirits and immaterial souls) can instantiate functional states (and that they must instantiate such states if they have minds) seems to indicate that functionalism is not an exclusively materialist position as has been claimed. This notion of spirit employed by those who believe that it might realize functional organization, however, is one that few, if any, thinkers who actually believe in spirits could embrace. Thomas Aquinas, for example, clearly believes that there are angels, that is, disembodied spirits or immaterial substances. However, it is also clear that he could not hold that they are subjects of functional states for the simple reason that they are simple, that is, being nonmaterial substances, they have no extension in space, and thus no discrete parts that can be organized into configurations or states.[30] Since something must have parts in order to realize a functional organization, Aquinas's view of spirits is incompatible with their having a functional organization. Since Aquinas also believes that his angels have mental states, that is, they know things, functionalist descriptions would not apply to angelic mentality. While angelic minds are admittedly a speculative conjecture (like Martians and Asimovian robots), this observation does something to temper functionalists' claims to a universal theory of mentality.

Aquinas's real reason for opposing functionalism, however, would come from the fact that functional states come to be and pass away in the manner of material transmutations, and he insists that coming to have mental states is not that kind of a change. When considering whether the human soul is a material reality, he explains why someone might think it is. Such thinkers believe "wherever there is found the properties of matter, it is necessary to find matter. Wherefore, since in the soul there is found the properties of matter which are to receive, to be subject, to be in potency and other such things, it is thought necessary that in the soul there be matter."[31] Thus, because activities of soul seem to be the sorts of activities that material things undergo, the soul seems to be a material thing. If the mind receives information or goes through a reasoning process, its reception and processing seem to indicate that it is made of matter into which it receives its information, and so forth.

It seems that Aquinas would see the general functionalist position as an analogous case. According to Aquinas, when a material thing undergoes a change, it implies the destruction of the prior state by a contrary one. This seems to be implied by a functionalist description of mental states, for the prior mental state causes subsequent mental states. However, in doing so the system ceases to be in that prior state. Thus, while functionalism defines each mental state by the causal role it plays in bringing about behavior or other mental states, it also entails that each mental state causes other states of a system and is replaced by those contrary states. The process of coming to be in a given functional state, and likewise the process of ceasing to be in that state, are transmutations of the physical system whose functional state it is. Aquinas declares that the reasoning that gives rise to a notion of souls composed of matter and form "is frivolous and the position is impossible;" he would have a similar assessment of the functionalist description of mental states.

The reason for this harsh judgment is that, although both material things and the soul are said to receive, to undergo and to be affected, each is said to do so for different reasons. To undergo a change in a material way is to be altered, that is, to have one affection or state replaced by another, contrary state. Aquinas, however, believes that coming to possess knowledge does not consist in being altered. "The soul, however, does not receive with motion and transmutation, but through separation from motion and movable things."[32] Coming to be in a mental state, then, is not the destruction of some prior state, but rather the fulfillment and completion of the knowing power. It remains to be seen whether Aquinas has good reason for thinking that this is what having a mental state consists in. For the present, it is clear that Aquinas believes that spiritual mental states are not transmutations. As such, they cannot be functional states of spirits. Functionalism, then, is a thoroughly materialist theory for the mind.

It is in their theory's stress on functional organization, however, that these sorts of materialists see an affinity with Aristotle, for they believe that this is what he means by form. Although in its ordinary use "form" connotes shape or configuration, Martha Nussbaum, for instance, claims that what Aristotle means by form is something very close to what functionalists mean by "functional organization."

But in the case of living things, it is very clear that to explain behavior we must refer not to surface configuration, but to the functional organization that the individuals share with other members of their species. This is the form; this, and not the shape remains the same as long as the creature is the same creature. The lion may change its shape, get thin or fat, without ceasing to be the same lion; its form is not its shape, but [is] its soul, the set of vital capacities, the functional organization, in virtue of which it lives and acts. . . . A corpse has the same *shape* as a living man; but it is not a man, since it cannot perform the activities appropriate to a man (PA 640b30–641a17). When I ask for the formal account of lion behavior, I am not, then, asking just for a reference to tawny color or great weight. I am asking for an account of what it is to be a lion: how lions are organized to function, what vital capacities they have, and how these interact. And it is this, again, rather than an enumeration of its material constituents, that will provide the most simple, general, and relevant account for the scientist interested in explaining and predicting lion behavior. (cf. PA 641a7–17)[33]

Neither Aristotle nor the modern functionalist believes that a reduction to material constituents provides an adequate explanation of animal behavior. An adequate explanation, however, can be given, it is argued, in terms of form for Aristotle or in terms of functional organization for the functionalist. It is further argued that Aristotle's form is equivalent to functional organization in all relevant aspects.

An essential point of the functionalist position is that the same functional states can be realized in a number of material systems. By claiming that Aristotle's form is functional organization, the issue of physiology (whether it is Aristotle's ancient account or contemporary medicine and biology's modern account) does not determine the truth or falsity of the functionalist theory. A functionalist interpretation of Aristotle is thus believed to make Aristotle relevant by showing his conformity with a contemporary philosophy of mind, while at the same time freeing his theory from the details of his outmoded biological views. One can thus claim to be essentially an Aristotelian (in virtue of the fact that he is a functionalist) while at the same time rejecting many of the details of his theory.

S. Marc Cohen claims that Aristotle is sympathetic to this feature of functionalism wherein the same mental states are realizable in various ways. According to Cohen, in *De Partibus Animalium*, Aristotle's

remarks strongly suggest a conviction that the same psychic state may have different material realizations. In animals made of flesh, for example, the organ of touch is flesh; in other animals it is the part "analogous to flesh" (PA 2. 1, 647a21). Sensations of touch occur in the flesh of humans, but in different (though analogous) organs of other species. Such observations, which abound throughout the work, suggest a sympathy for the *compositional plasticity* that is characteristic of functionalism.[34]

While admitting that it is not clear whether Aristotle believes that rationality might be realized in some functionally organized thing other than a human being, Cohen believes that this possibility is at least conceivable to Aristotle and consistent with his hylomorphic theory. Cohen thus concludes that in all essential points, Aristotle is a functionalist.

So the key elements of a materialistic variety of functionalism appears to be present in Aristotle's account. Psychical faculties and states require some material embodiment, but not any particular kind of embodiment. Their definitions are always given in terms of form and function, never in terms of material composition. They are multiply realizable, in that the same faculty or state may be found in different kinds of creatures with significantly different physiological make-ups.[35]

Functionalist interpreters believe, then, that Aristotle's theory provides just the pre-Cartesian medicine to heal philosophy of the mind-body dichotomy. Aristotle, while enjoying a richer notion of soul, is untainted by Descartes's distortion of soul into immaterial, unextended mind. Instead, he is still a materialist by virtue of being a functionalist. Aristotle's version of soul as "substance in the sense of being the form of a natural body, which potentially has life" (412a20–21),[36] according to this interpretation, could not survive the destruction of the body since it is simply the body's functional organization.

Aristotle's doctrine of νοῦς, however, presents a problem for his materialist interpreters. While there seems to be a *prima facie* case that Aristotle's account of animal behavior may be an ancient precursor to modern functionalist theory, his theory of what is distinctive of human thinking, that is, νοῦς, does not seem to fit with this materialist theory. For he says in a number of places that νοῦς is unmixed with the body or separate from it. While Aristotle might be a functionalist when it comes to animal minds, it seems he cannot be when it comes to human minds since he does not seem to be a materialist when it comes to νοῦς. Michael Wedin, however, attempts to give a materialist interpretation of Aristotle's doctrine of νοῦς by claiming that Aristotle, in fact, espouses a doctrine that in its essentials is a species of general functionalist theory, that is, cognitivism. In order to understand Wedin's interpretation, then, one must grasp the basic claims of cognitivism.

COGNITIVISM

Cognitivism is another contemporary theory designed to overcome the mind/body dichotomy inherited from Descartes. Like more generally functionalist theories of which it is a species, cognitivism is opposed to reductive materialism, which claims that psychological or intentional behavior can be explained directly by physiological processes and states. Cognitivists, like functionalists generally, define mental states in terms of the causal roles they play, as resulting from stimuli or other mental states (or both) and as causing other mental states or behavior (or both).

Cognitivists, however, go beyond simple functionalists by seeking explanations of overt behavior in varying levels of internal states. Developed as a reaction to psychological behaviorists' neglect of mental states in the explanation of human behavior, cognitivism affirms the relevance of discussing such internal states and accords them a significant and complex role in psychological theories.

Cognitivism is roughly the view that (i) psychologists may and must advert to inner states and episodes in explaining behavior, so long as the states and episodes are construed throughout as physical, and (ii) human beings and other psychological organisms are best viewed as in some sense information-processing systems. As cognitive psychology sets the agenda, its questions take the form "How does this organism receive information through its sense-organs, process the information, store it, and then mobilize it in such a way as to result in intelligent behavior?"[37]

Cognitivism as a species of functionalism shares with its generic theory a commitment to materialism, in that the organisms whose internal states it postulates and seeks to define are entirely physical things. Moreover, like more general versions of functionalism, cognitivism claims that the matter out of which such organisms are made is not what accounts for their exhibiting mental properties, but rather it is the fact that that matter is organized in such a way that its physical states are caused by appropriate stimuli or other internal states and cause appropriate behavior and other internal states. "[C]ognitivism thinks of human beings as systems of interconnected functional components, interacting with each other in an efficient and productive way."[38]

For cognitivists, however, in addition to basic functional states that are directly realized in the physical makeup of a system or organism, there are also higher-level states that result from lower-level states having a certain functional organization of their own. Not only are there functional states that directly result from the matter of an organism being organized such that these states result from stimuli and other states and issue in other states and in behavior, but there are several levels of such states, with higher levels of states being the functional organization of lower-level ones. Observable behavior, then, is explained in terms of the various levels of states and organization.[39] Thus, cognitivists appeal to the functional organization of a system's structures or "hardware," in order to explain mental states, but hold that these states themselves have a functional organization that constitutes higher-level mental states. For example, a cognitivist would claim that there are basic states in sensation, such as the states that seeing white and tasting sweet consist in. These states are themselves organized into higher-level states. Thus, the internal states that are sensations of sweet and white may be organized or connected so that the perception of sugar results at a higher level of organization. This experience of sugar, then, may be part of an even higher functional state of recollecting an event of eating sugar or of desiring to eat it in the future. What is characteristic of cognitivism is that it postulates a variety of levels of functional organization and thus a variety of levels of functional states. The whole system, however, is reducible to the hardware and the functional organization that it realizes, allowing, of course, that other hardware may realize the same various levels of organization and resultant states.

When Michael Wedin comes to interpreting Aristotle's theory of mind, he invokes the cognitivist understanding of mentality, claiming that Aristotle, at least in spirit, endorses cognitivist explanations. According to Wedin, Aristotle's description and explanation of φαντασία and νοῦς are consistent with a cognitivist characterization of them as a higher-level functional organization of more basic physical states, for example, the states of sense organs becoming affected by their proper objects. In claiming Aristotle is a cognitivist, Wedin thereby affirms that Aristotle is a materialist even in his doctrine of νοῦς, despite the fact that in a number of texts Aristotle says that νοῦς is separate from the body or that it is apart from matter. Wedin, then, offers an interpretation of Aristotle's doctrine of νοῦς that is at once cognitivist but denies that Aristotle really meant that mind is separate in any strong sense.

SUPERVENIENCE

One problem that has been seen with functionalism is that it does not accord enough of a role to the introspectible, phenomenal character of mental states. For, on the functionalist explanation of mentality, one could have all the mental states that functional theory specifies, and in the way it specifies them, but have very different mental states according to their phenomenal character, or have states with no phenomenal character whatsoever. In the latter case, it seems entirely conceivable that a system or organism may be functionally isomorphic to a normal human being (its internal states cause behavior and other states and are caused by stimuli and other states, just as a psychological theory specifies), but have no phenomenal features to its mental states. Such a creature, devoid of consciousness, is popularly (and in the professional literature) known as a "zombie."[40] A zombie may have the functional state of pain, but it does not hurt; the zombie just acts like it does. Any theory that allows that zombies may have mental states identical to a human's, it is believed, must be flawed.

For this reason, mental properties are sometimes declared to be irreducible to the physical properties of the organisms that have them, but mental properties are nevertheless said to depend on, and be totally determined by, the physical properties. Mental properties are thus said to *supervene* on physical properties. Jaegwon Kim explains the notion of supervenience by asking his reader to consider the relation between a marble sculpture one is creating and its aesthetic beauty. Sculpting, Kim notes, is laborious work by which one endows the marble block with certain physical properties, for example, shape and texture. The aesthetic properties, however, are not some additional properties requiring some other kind of work.

When the physical work has been finished, there is no *further* aesthetic work to do, no further step of attaching beauty and other desired aesthetic properties to the material object you have created. Once the physical work is done the whole project is done. This is so because the physical properties of the object wholly determine its aesthetic properties. And we may justify the attribution of an aesthetic property to it on the basis of the physical properties on which it supervenes (e.g., it is beautiful and expressive because its physical shape, texture, etc. are thus and so). In this sense, aesthetic properties of an object or situation *supervene* on its physical properties.[41]

Sometimes supervenience is explained by saying that supervening properties will be the same when the things on which they supervene are the same. Thus, if aesthetic properties supervene on physical properties, then "any two works of art that are physically indiscernable must of necessity be aesthetically indiscernable."[42] This notion of supervenience is likewise applied to the relation between mind and matter. As aesthetic properties of beauty and expressiveness supervene on, that is, are determined by but not reducible to, the physical properties of shape and texture, so mental properties, like having a sharp pain, supervene on, that is, are determined by but not reducible to, physical properties, like having C-fibers fire.

Stephen Everson utilizes the notion of supervenience when he gives his own interpretation of Aristotle's doctrine of perception. Everson claims that, for Aristotle, perception as cognitive awareness supervenes on physical processes that take place in sense organs.[43] As such, he accepts the definition of supervenience given by Donald Davidson. "Such supervenience might be taken to mean that there cannot be two events alike in all physical respects but differing in some mental respect, or that an object cannot alter in some mental respect without altering in some physical respect."[44] Supervenience, then, essentially exploits the weakness of material implication ($p \rightarrow q$), for it claims that if the mental changes, then the physical must have changed, but that the physical can change without the mental necessarily changing. Furthermore, there may be more than one physical state associated with a given mental state, such that an animal can have the same mental state while certain of its physical features change. If it or another animal is in the same physical state, however, then it will be, by that very fact, in the associated mental state—that is, for every mental property, if something has that mental property, then it has a certain physical property, such that whatever has that physical property will then have the mental one as well.[45] According to Everson, the mental state of being aware of a red object supervenes, in Aristotle's theory, on the physical alteration the eye undergoes in receiving the form of red without the object's matter. Awareness is not reducible to the physical alteration, but it is nevertheless determined by it. Aristotle thus appears to be relevant to contemporary discussions about the relation between mind and body by again being identified as an ancient precursor to a non-reductivist, yet thoroughly materialist, theory of mind.

CONCLUSION

With an overview of Descartes's dichotomy between mind and body, as well as various reactions against it that shape contemporary philosophy of mind, one can now understand the influence of these various positions on contemporary interpretations of Aristotle. Although Aristotle's psychological theory lends itself to being assimilated to neither Cartesian dualism nor reductive materialism, proponents of materialist theories, reacting against these prior alternatives, have sought an ally in Aristotle. As the principal reaction to reductive materialism, functionalism is seen to have many points in common with Aristotle's hylomorphism. Attempts at asserting full compatibility between Aristotle's theory and functionalism, however, appear to be thwarted by Aristotle's contention that the intellect is separate from the body. Wedin tries to overcome this apparent incongruity by enlisting the cognitive variety of functionalism into his interpretive strategy. An evaluation of Wedin's interpretation will be the focus of the next chapter. Another reaction to reductive materialism, as well as to functionalism, the claim that mental states are irreducible to, yet nevertheless supervene on, physical states is likewise alleged by Everson to have an affinity with Aristotle's theory of perception. Everson's claims will be explored in Chapter 4. Wedin's and Everson's interpretations, however, are also the chief obstacles to providing an explanation of the cogency of Aristotle's arguments in *DA* 3.4. Cognitivist functionalism and supervenience, then, figure into the overall argument of this book as the contemporary (materialist) framework for denying that Aristotle proves that the intellect is a nonmaterial power. Hence, this survey of contemporary theories serves as an explanatory background to these interpretations by placing them in their own conceptual context.

NOTES

1. René Descartes, *Meditations Concerning First Philosophy*, tr. Laurence J. Lafleur (Indianapolis: Bobbs-Merrill Co., Inc., 1960), p. 82.

2. Ibid., p. 84.

3. Ibid., p. 132.

4. Jaegwon Kim, *Philosophy of Mind* (Boulder, CO: Westview Press, 1996), p. 4.

5. Ibid., p. 211.

6. Ibid., p. 57.

7. Paul M. Churchland, *Matter and Consciousness* (Cambridge, MA: MIT Press, 1984), p. 26.

8. Kim, *Philosophy of Mind*, p. 57.

9. Ibid., p. 212.

10. Churchland, *Matter and Consciousness*, p. 27.

11. The kind of reduction characteristic of harmony theory should be distinguished from functionalist claims that the soul is, or results from, the arrangement of a thing's material constituents.

12. Charles H. Kahn, "Aristotle on Thinking," in *Essays on Aristotle's.* De Anima, ed. Martha C. Nussbaum and Amélie Oksenberg Rorty (Oxford: Clarendon Press, 1992), p. 359.

13. S. Marc Cohen, "Hylomorphism and Functionalism," in *Essays on Aristotle's*, De Anima, ed. Martha C. Nussbaum and Amélie Oksenberg Rorty (Oxford: Clarendon Press, 1992) p. 57.

14. Churchland, *Matter and Consciousness*, p. 36.

15. The fact that a functionalist conception of mind or soul does not depend on the specific material constituents of whatever physical system it is realized in distinguishes it from the theory that the soul is a harmony of bodily elements. Functionalism maintains that the matter whose organization allows it to function in mentalistic ways need not be of a specific type, but it need only have certain properties on account of which it has the appropriate, that is, functionally specified, causal relations. The harmony theory against which Aristotle argues, however, reasons that the soul results from certain elements in a certain proportion. See Michael Frede, "On Aristotle's Conception of Soul," in *Essays on Aristotle's* De Anima, ed. Martha C. Nussbaum and Amélie Oksenberg Rorty (Oxford: Clarendon Press, 1992), pp. 98–99.

16. Churchland, *Matter and Consciousness*, p. 37.

17. Hilary Putnam, "Brains and Behavior," in *Readings in Philosophy of Psychology*, ed. Ned Block (Cambridge, MA: Harvard University Press, 1980), p. 36.

18. Churchland, *Matter and Consciousness*, p. 38.

19. Hilary Putnam, "Philosophy and Our Mental Life," in *Readings in Philosophy of Psychology*, ed. Ned Block (Cambridge, MA: Harvard University Press, 1980), p. 134.

20. Ibid., p. 136.

21. Ibid.

22. Ned Block, "What Is Functionalism?" in *Readings in Philosophy of Psychology*, ed. Ned Block (Cambridge, MA: Harvard University Press, 1980), p. 174; see also ibid. pp. 175, 180.

23. Ibid.

24. Ibid., p. 175.

25. Ibid., p. 180; see also, ibid., p. 181.

26. They are unspecified because we will want to say that they can be realized in humans, lions, Martians and so forth.

27. Richard Boyd, "Materialism without Reductionism: What Physicalism Does Not Entail," in Readings *in Philosophy of Psychology*, ed. Ned Block (Cambridge, MA: Harvard University Press, 1980), p. 101.

28. Block, "What Is Functionalism?" p. 181; see also Putnam, "Philosophy and Our Mental Life," p. 142.

29. Hilary Putnam, "Why Functionalism Didn't Work," in *Words and Life*, ed. James Conant (Cambridge, MA: Harvard University Press, 1994), p. 441.

30. Thomas Aquinas, *Opera Omnia*, iussu Leonis XIII P. M. edita, Tomus V, *Summa Theologiae* Ia, q. 52, a. 1, cura et studio Fratrum Predicatorum (Romae: Ex Typographia Polyglotta S. C. de Propoganda Fide, 1889), p. 20. Corpus enim est in loco per hoc, quod applicatur loco secundum contactum dimensivae quantitatis. Quae quidem in angelis non est; sed est in eis quantitas virtualis.

31. Thomas Aquinas, *Quaestio disputata* de Anima, a. 6, in *Quaestions Disputatae*, ed. P. Caramello (Taurini: Marietti, 1965), p. 301. Huius autem ratio est, quae etiam in obiieciendo est tacta, quod oportet in quocumque inveniuntur proprietates materiae, inveniri materiam. Unde cum in anima inveniantur proprietates materiae, quae sunt recipere, subiici, esse in potentia, et alia huiusmodi; arbitratur esse necessarium quod in anima sit materia.

32. Anima autem non recipit cum motu et transmutatione, immo per separationem a moti et a rebus mobilis. Ibid.

33. *Aristotle's* De Motu Animalium: *Text with Translation, Commentary, and Interpretive Essays*, Essay 1 ed. Martha Nussbaum (Princeton: Princeton University Press, 1978), p. 71.

34. Cohen, "Hylomorphism," p. 59.

35. Ibid., p. 60.

36. ἀνάγκαιον ἄρα τὴν ψυχὴν οὐσίαν εἶναι ὡς εἶδος σώματος φυσικοῦ δυνάμει ζωὴν ἔχοντος.

37. William G. Lycan, "Functionalism (1)," in *A Companion to the Philosophy of Mind*, ed. Samuel Guttenplan (Oxford: Blackwell Publishers, 1994), p. 319.

38. Ibid.

39. Wedin, *Mind and Imagination in Aristotle*, p. 2.

40. Kim, *Philosophy of Mind*, p. 169.

41. Ibid., p. 222.

42. Ibid.

43. Stephen Everson, *Aristotle on Perception* (Oxford: Clarendon Press, 1997).

44. Ibid., p. 259. See Donald Davidson, "Mental Events," in *Essays on Actions and Events, ed. Donald Davidson* (Oxford: Oxford University Press, 1980).

45. Everson, *Aristotle on Perception*, p. 263. Everson, in fact, believes that Aristotle holds to a stronger version of supervenience where a bi-conditional obtains between the mental and the physical, such that one is in a given mental state if and only if one is in the associated physical state (cf. pp. 279–280).

CHAPTER 2

The Separability of Νοῦς and Cognitivist Functionalism

INTRODUCTION

Aristotle's doctrine of νοῦς in the *De Anima* has received quite varied reactions, especially from functionalists. There are many who have no trouble viewing what Aristotle has to say on the intellect (or on the senses for that matter) as an endorsement of dualism.[1] K. V. Wilkes regards Aristotle's comments on the mind in the *De Anima* as an embarrassment to his otherwise thoroughly materialist account of mental capacities and functions.[2] Thus, while she believes that the immateriality of the mind, for which Aristotle argues, is not a theory that any committed dualist would embrace, nevertheless, she wishes that he had never written the troublesome lines.[3] Deborah Modrak seems willing to view the doctrine of these chapters as integral to Aristotle's overall theory, but as posing no serious threat to his commitment to embodied minds.[4] The metaphysical status of νοῦς in *DA* 3.4, then, does not enjoy a settled interpretation, even among functionalists.

Michael Wedin, in *Mind and Imagination in Aristotle*,[5] has adopted what is perhaps the most radical interpretation of Aristotle's doctrine of νοῦς. For Wedin, Aristotle's commitment to his own hylomorphic theory precludes the possibility that νοῦς acts apart from matter. Despite textual appearances and a long tradition of commentary and interpretation to the contrary, Wedin does not believe that Aristotle held that the intellect or any part of the soul acts separately from the body. Accordingly, he offers an interpretation of *De Anima* wherein Aristotle is a thoroughgoing materialist. Specifically, Aristotle's theory is an early version of the cognitivist variety of functionalism, according to Wedin. Not even Book 3, Chapter 4, nor the closely related Chapter 5, elicit from Wedin an admission that νοῦς enjoys any serious sort of independence from the body. He takes this extreme view because he believes that the general theory articulated in the *DA* cannot be made consistent with any claim that the mind acts apart from the body. For Wedin such a claim amounts to a dualism of the sort advocated by Plato or Descartes.

In order to fairly assess Aristotle's arguments in *DA* 3.4, however, one must first establish Aristotle's aims in this controversial part of the *DA*. If, as Wedin claims, Aristotle is not trying to show that the intellect exists or acts in a non-bodily way, then terms like "unmixed" and "separate," which seem to denote this sort of immateriality, will have to be interpreted in a correspondingly different light. If, however, Aristotle were, indeed, trying to demonstrate that the faculty of thought can exist apart from the body, then such an aim will give a correspondingly differing sense to these key terms. Moreover, the identification and import of the evidence advanced will depend on what intended conclusion the arguments seek to prove. For, it is unlikely that the same evidence could generate the conclusion that Wedin believes is intended, namely, that νοῦς is separate from any particular organ but not from the body altogether, and also generate a contrary conclusion. Success in evaluating *DA* 3.4, then, first requires success in determining Aristotle's intent.

However, in order to evaluate whether Aristotle's doctrine of νοῦς must succumb to Wedin's materialist interpretation of it, one must determine whether Aristotle's understanding of his hylomorphism precludes the possibility that some mental activities occur apart from the body. If Aristotle allows that mental activities may be separate from matter, one must further determine whether this sort of separation amounts to the sort of dualism analogous to the Platonic or Cartesian variety. My present goal is to determine whether Aristotle, in *DA* 3.4, seeks to show that νοῦς is separate from the body and what the nature of that separation is—that is, I hope to determine whether Aristotle intended his doctrine on the intellect to be a materialist theory. I evaluate Wedin's claim that, for Aristotle, νοῦς is a material power best explained in terms of the cognitivist variety of functionalism.

WEDIN'S MATERIALIST INTERPRETATION OF Νοῦς

Armed with the powerful explanatory model for the mind that the cognitivist variety of functionalism affords, Wedin notes the difficulty interpreters have had in trying to explain Aristotle's theory of the intellect. Most have tried either to present a coherent version attributing to νοῦς "transcendentalistic" qualities, on the one hand, or ignoring νοῦς, on the other.[6] Faced with this interpretive deadlock, Wedin proposes his own solution. Although the *De Anima* often calls the intellect separate (χωριστὸς) or claims that it is or acts without matter (ἄνευ τῆς ὕλης), Wedin reads these passages according to what he calls a "finitistic" interpretation.

Strong and Weak Separation

Wedin's distinction between transcendentalistic and finitistic accounts of νοῦς corresponds to two senses in which the intellect might be separate from matter or the body, strong and weak respectively. Strong separation, or what Wedin refers to as transcendentalistic properties, would belong to the intellect were it a substance in itself, distinct from the substance of the body. Thus, dualists favor strong separation. Indeed, a dualist such as Howard Robinson believes that the strong separation of νοῦς is the simplest way to show that Aristotle is a dualist.[7]

Straightforward dualism is not the only way of conceiving strong separation. Strong separation would also belong to the intellect if it were not a substance in its own right, but rather a power of the soul whose operations are not simultaneously the operations of any part of the body. While the intellect might always, and only, belong to a bodily creature, nevertheless, if the activity proper to the intellect is not realized in any part or collection of parts of the body, it would count as separate in a strong sense, though perhaps not as strong a sense as that of a separate substance. I hope to show that Aristotle advocates this sort of strong separation and so resists simple classification as a dualist. For ease of reference, "separate$_s$" or "separation$_s$" will signify both versions of strong separation.

On the other hand, weak separation, that is, what Wedin calls a finitistic account, applies to any conception of the intellect as essentially and necessarily realized in a bodily creature. As separate in a weak sense, the mind depends upon and results from a complex of cognitive capacities that are themselves directly realized in bodily structures. For Wedin, the mind is separate from certain bodily powers, for example, the senses and imagination, in the sense that it is not identical with these lower powers. However, the mind so conceived is separate in a merely weak sense, because it cannot occur without the sense faculties or the physical structures on which these faculties depend, and its activity is the coordinated activity of various parts of the body. Although it is not realized in its own bodily structures in the way that sense powers are realized in their organs, nevertheless, the mind in a way results from these lower faculties, and so it is realized in the body as a whole, but not in any one part. When the lower-level faculties cease, or when the physical structures that give rise to the lower faculties are destroyed, so the higher faculty of mind is thereby destroyed. Weak separation accordingly precludes the possibility of immortality. For ease of reference, "separate$_w$" or "separation$_w$" will signify weak separation.

In connection with claims about the strong separation of the intellect, one should note two points. First, strong separation of the intellect should not be understood to mean necessarily that the intellect is actually disembodied—that is, the claim that the intellect is separate$_s$ from the body does not mean that a person's intellect is now unconnected with a body or that it is associated with an embodied person in a merely incidental way. At least some versions of the strong separation of the intellect are meant to apply to embodied, living human beings who engage in intellectual activity. Thus, to claim that the intellect is separate$_s$ from the body does not commit one to denying that the intellects of living human beings are united to their bodies. Some who claim that the intellect is separate$_s$ also seek to assert that human beings are single substances, having a physical body that is nevertheless united to a separate$_s$ intellect. Their claim is merely that the intellectual activity of embodied persons occurs by means of a power that is not itself embodied, but is thus separate$_s$.

The second point to note about the intellect's strong separation is its relation to a claim about immortality. Strong separation, while significantly related to immortality, is not identical with it. Even though the ability to survive the death of the body may be a consequence of strong separation, such survival is not directly what is meant by saying that the intellect is separate$_S$. The only necessary connection that obtains between separation and immortality is a negative one for weak separation, for the ability to survive the destruction of the body could not belong to an intellect that is separate$_W$. Strong separation is a necessary condition for the intellect to be immortal, while weak separation precludes immortality.

Wedin on the Weak Separation of Νοῦς

Wedin believes that weak separation fits better with Aristotle's general definition of the soul and his psychophysical explanation of animate activity, as well as with specific texts from the *DA*. As Deborah Modrak explains, a separate$_S$ νοῦς seems to engender untoward consequences for a comprehensive Aristotelian psychology: "If the definition of soul (ψυχή) applies only to faculties that enform specific bodily systems, then *nous qua* faculty for thinking will fall outside the purview of the definition and thus *nous* will not be a constituent of the soul."[8] Whereas some interpreters choose to write off the doctrine of νοῦς as not essential to Aristotle's whole psychological theory, Wedin's solution to such problems is to deny that νοῦς is separate in any strong sense. In order to establish this view of νοῦς, however, he must offer a consistent interpretation of many texts from *DA*, and not only those found in Book 3. His ability to do so will determine the success of his interpretation. As will become clear, the notion of strong separation against which Wedin argues is what might be called super-strong separation, the mind as a separate substance. What should also become clear is that his interpretation of νοῦς as material fails when texts from outside Book 3 are seen in the light of another sense of strong separation. This latter sense of strong separation is the sense in which Aristotle intended to cast an understanding of νοῦς as acting apart from the body.

In interpreting Aristotle as a cognitivist, Wedin believes that νοῦς is separate$_W$ and so part of an overall materialist theory of the mind. Thus, he believes that Aristotle develops his account of νοῦς in order to avoid postulating any nonmaterial entities.[9] For Wedin, Aristotle indicates his sympathy with this sort of cognitivistic explanation of the senses and imagination by saying that these faculties are related to their organs as form is to matter (412b18–20). Thus, these faculties are the actualization of the physical structures that are their organs, and the faculties are thus directly realized in these structures; sense faculties are not separate at all from the body. However, when Aristotle says that mind is separate, he merely means that it has no physical structures peculiar to itself. It emerges, as it were, from the faculties that do have their own structures in which they are realized and of which they are the organization. Therefore, νοῦς is a higher-level function requiring lower-level ones, but it is not identical with them. A thought, while not the same as an image, requires the use of an image in order to be represented to the person thinking it.[10] Mind results from such sense faculties (imagination, in particular, as an internal representational state) being organized in such a way as to enable intelligent behavior to arise. As the other faculties are the forms of their organs, so mind is the form of these faculties. While other faculties are realized in their organs, mind is not so directly realized, but results from the organization of these other, lower faculties.[11] Thus, for Wedin, νοῦς is separate in that it has no simple realization in bodily structures; νοῦς is separate$_w$ in that it still has a physical realization as a higher-level functional organization.

Wedin's interpretation of νοῦς in *DA* 3 accordingly presents the faculty of thought in cognitivist terms, and *prima facie* he makes a plausible case. Central to Wedin's interpretation is Aristotle's statement that mind is nothing actual before it thinks.

T1a[12]: It is necessary that, since mind thinks all things, it should be "unmixed," as Anaxagoras says, in order that it may be "in control," that is, that it may know; for anything appearing inwardly hinders and obstructs what is foreign. Hence the mind, too, can have no characteristic except its capacity to receive. (429a18–22)[13]

T1b: That part of the soul which we call mind (by mind I mean that part by which the soul thinks and forms judgments) is nothing actual until it thinks. So it is unreasonable to suppose that it is mixed with the body; for in that case it would become somehow qualitative (ποιός τις γὰρ ἂν γίγνοιτο), e.g., as hot or cold, or would even have some organ, as the sensitive faculty has; but as it is it has none. (429a22–25)[14]

For Wedin, this passage means that, while Aristotle's description of the mind mirrors his method of defining other cognitive faculties in terms of their functions, mind differs from the senses in that it has no physical structures of which it is the actuality. Lest Wedin's readers think that he believes voῦς is separate$_s$, in a note he asserts: "Thus, Aristotle is here not claiming . . . that mind is *completely* independent of the body. See 429a22–25 which implies that were a faculty mixed with the body, it will be something actual prior to thinking, namely the structure or structures over which it is defined (of which it is the actualization)."[15] Apparently for Wedin, when Aristotle says at 429a22–25 that the faculty of thought cannot be a mixed power since it then would be something actual, he is endorsing weak separation.

Wedin's citation of T1b from *DA* 3.4 alone, however, is not conclusive support for weak separation. Clearly, T1b claims that a faculty with structure(s) has a prior actuality that disqualifies it as the faculty of thinking. However, such a claim seems to be required of, or is at least compatible with, a notion of voῦς that is separate in either sense, weak or strong—that is, if 429a22–25 says that the unmixed character of voῦς means that it has no physical structure or structures of which it is the first actualization, then this feature applies to both strong and weak separation. Therefore, it is not evidence that mind is separate$_w$, as Wedin believes.

The fact that Wedin believes 429a22–25 implies the conditional "if x is mixed with the body, x is actual prior to thinking" shows he is misreading Aristotle's argument. First of all, Wedin apparently does not see the two parts of the chapter as constituting one argument, for he refers only to the latter section, that is, T1b. Furthermore, he seems to read T1b as saying that voῦς being "nothing actual" until it thinks entails that it is not mixed with the body. For were it so mixed with the body, it would have some quality such as hot or cold in virtue of its organ, and thus have an actuality prior to thinking, that is, the actuality of the organ. Being mixed with the body is just to have an organ that entails having a temperature.

It seems a little shortsighted for Wedin to believe that Aristotle thinks that being unmixed with the body is a consequence only of the intellect's having no actuality prior to thought since the passage allegedly asserting this, T1b, is not the first time that Aristotle draws the inference that voῦς is unmixed. In T1a, Aristotle claims that the reason that the intellect is unmixed is that it knows all things, and thus has nothing appearing inwardly (παρεμφαινόμενον). To have nothing appear inwardly is at least part of what it means to be unmixed, and this is also equivalent to saying that the intellect has no other nature than a capacity.

Likewise, being only a capacity, it has no actuality prior to thought. Aristotle next takes up the counter-factual claim that if the intellect were mixed with the body, its activity would mirror that of the senses, which become somehow qualitative, a consequence of the fact that they have organs.

Aristotle's point in T1b, then, is not to show how the claim that νοῦς is unmixed follows from having no actuality prior to thought as Wedin thinks. Rather, he seems to intend to trace the absurd consequences of saying that mind is not unmixed, that is, that it is mixed with the body. If mind were a physical actuality prior to thinking, it would become hot or cold, that is, its activity would consist in the coming to be of a quality, hence the importance of saying it would *become* somehow qualitative (ποιός τις γὰρ ἂν γίγνοιτο). Aristotle, in the following line, seems to be making the further point (apparently an empirical observation) that mind has no organ, which it also would have if it were mixed with the body. Coming to have some quality like temperature, then, is not an immediate consequence of having an organ. Rather, the coming to be of some quality (to which the faculty of thought is immune) is the kind of process that something having an organ would undergo. And such a process is incompatible with Aristotle's understanding of the activity of thinking only because he had previously sketched his understanding of that activity as already implying that νοῦς is unmixed. Thus, having no actuality prior to thought is not the reason that intellect is unmixed, as Wedin's reading implies. Being unmixed is instead the reason that mind has no actuality prior to thought, and also why its activity is not a case of "becoming somehow qualitative" as is the activity of those faculties that have organs.

The opposition between sense and intellect that Aristotle seems to be establishing actually militates against Wedin's interpretation. One should remember that he interprets the mind's separation and unmixedness as separation$_w$, that is, as the characteristic of a higher-level cognitive faculty than the senses. In fact, there are many such higher-level faculties for Wedin, φαντασία being the one that occupies most of his attention, and each of them is also without any specific bodily realization. Imagination depends on the body, for instance, in a general way, but it is not tied to the operation of any particular sense organ.[16] It is bodily insofar as it is a higher-level cognitive function of a bodily cognitive system, but it has no specific organ. For Aristotle, however, imagination is realized in the same part or parts of an animal as the sense faculty (αἰσθητικόν) is.

But since we have discussed imagination in the treatise *On the Soul*, and the imaginative (φανταστικόν) is the same as the sensitive faculty (αἰσθητικῷ), although the imaginative and sensitive are different in essence; . . . it is clear that dreaming belongs to the sensitive faculty, but belongs to it *qua* imaginative. (*Ins* 1.459a15–18, 22)[17]

Moreover, in T1b Aristotle describes the αἰσθητικόν as ὄργανόν, that is, as possessing an organ, and contrasts this with mind being un-mixed. Therefore, φαντασία and νοῦς do not have the same relation to the body according to Aristotle. Wedin's interpretation of νοῦς as separate$_w$, however, implies that they should, and to the extent this im-plication is blocked by Aristotle's contrast in T1b, Wedin's interpretation is seriously compromised.

Having interpreted 3.4 as favoring weak separation, Wedin goes on to consider certain key passages in 3.5 along the same interpretive line. Wedin's cognitivist interpretation sees 3.5 as offering the mechanisms whereby νοῦς effects the features that in 3.4 were said to be characteristic of thinking. Moreover, as the generic account of νοῦς in 3.4 concerns a faculty separate$_w$, so the mechanisms that 3.5 posits to explain it are separate$_w$. Thus, on the basis of his interpretation of 3.4, Wedin simply claims that the passages of 3.5 that seem to favor strong separation, in fact, do not. For instance, 3.5 claims:

T2: This mind [productive mind] is (a) separable and (b) not capable of being affected and (c) unmixed since (d) in its being it is activity. (430a17–18)[18]

According to Wedin, if a refers to ontological independence, it does not threaten Aristotle's materialism.

Given that a is grouped with b and c, the notion of separation here awarded productive mind is too weak to support a Cartesian notion of mind, let alone a doctrine of pre- or postexistence. For suppose that b and c refer back to *De Anima* 3.4's arguments for the independence of mind. Can we now take these arguments to pertain to productive mind? Recall that the mentioned arguments show only that mind is independent of the body in the sense that mind is not the actualization$_1$ of any set of physical structures.[19]

Because he thinks he has shown that T1 supports weak separation, Wedin feels he is free to dismiss any strong sense of separation attaching to T2. The weak separation of productive mind, then, hangs on the strength of his interpretation of "separate" in 3.4.

Likewise, when Wedin turns to what appears to be Aristotle's most explicit declaration that νοῦς is separate_s, he predictably relies on his earlier interpretation. In *DA* 3.5, Aristotle declares:

T3: (i) When separated [χωρισθεὶς] it is just that very thing that it is [μόνον τοῦθ ὅπερ ἐστί] and this alone [τοῦτο μόνον] is (j) not capable of death [ἀθάνατον] and is (k) eternal [ἀΐδιον].(430a22–23)[20]

Admitting that this passage poses a greater challenge to his interpretation, Wedin appeals to a grammatical difference in this declaration of separation.[21] Wedin believes that Aristotle's deliberate use of the aorist participle is required for a nuanced sense of separation because another use of χωριστός would have been repetitive of his claims in T2 and, thus, insufficient for some kind of immortality and eternity. Wedin, therefore, believes that χωρισθεὶς signifies an attenuated sense of immortality and eternality attaching to the abstract consideration of noetic activity apart from any content. Wedin believes that this different sort of separation is what Aristotle suggested was being "separate in thought" at the beginning of *DA* 3.4. On the assumption that changelessness is equivalent to immortality, Wedin sees Aristotle's account of νοῦς ποιητικός as parallel to the separation that the objects of mathematics enjoy, that is, the separation_w of abstractions.[22] Wedin's argument amounts to this: If χωριστός does not entail immortality and eternality, and χωρισθεὶς does, then χωρισθεὶς must have a different sense, but not one that entails any sort of strong separation for νοῦς since the abstract objects of mathematics also have similar characteristics while being merely separate_w. Therefore, χωρισθεὶς means "having been separated in thought"; the activity of thinking is immortal and eternal just to the extent that it has been separated in thought as an abstraction.

In response to Wedin's interpretation, the following points should be noted: First of all, Wedin's claim that unless Aristotle intends a different sense of separation in T3 he would be repeating himself is tenuous at best. The claim in T2 was that productive mind is separable (χωριστός) because (among other things) "in its being it is activity." In T3, however, the claim is that "it is just that very thing that it is," and it alone is deathless and eternal when separated (χωρισθεὶς). The difference between χωριστὸς and χωρισθεὶς need not be different senses of separation, weak versus abstract consideration, but may merely be the difference between a simple attribute and that attribute taken as the basis for other attributes. Even without fixing a precise meaning for "just that very thing that it is," it would not be repetitive of Aristotle to claim that the separation that productive mind enjoys because "in its being it is activity" is furthermore the *reason why* it is also immortal.

Second, Wedin's argument for the parallel between mathematical objects and νοῦς ποιητικός is predicated on the equivalence between immortality and changelessness. In fact, Aristotle almost never refers to anything other than a living being as immortal,[23] and "immortal" is even given as a *differentia* of "living."[24] The only exceptions concern the eternality of the infinite and of motion,[25] but in both these cases Aristotle is clearly considering ενδοξα, that is, the received opinion of his predecessors. At least in the case of the world's motion, he links the immortality of motion to the immortality of God.[26] "The activity of God is immortality, viz. eternal life. Therefore, the movement of God must be eternal" (*De Caelo* 2.3, 286a9–10). Indeed, if Aristotle meant that the activity of mind were an abstraction like mathematical objects, he would more likely have used imperishable (ἀφθαρτον).[27] The fact, then, that Aristotle includes ἀθάνατον in his description of the creative mind in T3 is enough to show that Wedin's ascription of separation_w on the basis of a similarity to the objects of mathematics is unfounded.

Finally, Wedin ultimately fails to give a justification for his claim that T3 requires a different sense of separation from the one used in T2. He had claimed that χωριστὸς in T2 failed to generate immortality and eternality, and since χωρισθεὶς does give rise to these attributes, the latter must mean "separate in thought." However, his reason why separation in T2 is weak is that it refers back to T1 in *DA* 3.4. However, that one text could be interpreted as favoring either strong or weak separation. Wedin, then, presents no conclusive evidence from Book 3 that νοῦς is a material power and separate only in a weak sense.

Even if one grants that Wedin can make a plausible case that νοῦς is susceptible to a cognitivist description, there is nothing in *DA* 3.4–5 that requires that an interpretation favoring weak separation is Aristotle's true intent. The question whether separation in *DA* 3 means strong separation or weak separation cannot be decided on the basis of these few passages alone since, as Wedin presents them, they all hang on *DA* 3.4 and this is open to either interpretation. The real work of justifying either kind of separation then will be done by appeal to passages outside of Book 3. Wedin attempts to do this as well.

The Requirements of Physics

Wedin's reason for believing that Aristotle did not intend to show that νοῦς is separate$_s$ is primarily that Aristotle's whole account of cognitive powers is committed to an embodied realization of such powers. Wedin takes it to be an essential feature of Aristotle's treatment of the soul in the *DA* that this study is part of physics, and a physical account of something includes both matter and form. Since the *DA* is part of physics, its account of the mental must include matter and form. Furthermore, since the treatment of νοῦς is part of *DA*, it also must be explained as composed of matter and form. Because of the requirements of Aristotle's methodology according to which Aristotle's account of cognitive powers is part of a physical investigation, Wedin believes that all of the *DA*, including the explanation of thinking in Book 3, is open to a cognitivist interpretation. Accordingly, Wedin claims that those passages that allegedly support an interpretation of νοῦς as separate$_s$ are amenable to his cognitivist interpretation.

In general, Wedin has good reason for thinking that it is Aristotle's position that whatever is studied in physics must be investigated as form in matter and that this is the true nature of Aristotle's explanation of natural things. He appropriately cites *Physics* 2.1–2 as support for this understanding.[28] Wedin, however, believes that this requirement of Aristotelian physics carries over to the study of soul and all its powers in a straightforward way. For Wedin, it is a principle of Aristotelian science that "the physicist is interested in forms that are *essentially realized* in some matter or other."[29] He believes, too, that this principle extends to Aristotelian psychology and accordingly cites *Metaphysics* (*Meta*) 6.1:

T4: It is clear also that it falls to the student of physics [φυσικοῦ] to investigate a certain sort of soul, namely whatever is not without matter [ὅση μὴ ἄνευ τῆς ὕλης]. (1026a5–6)[30]

According to Wedin, Aristotle here asserts that in order to be investigated by the physicist, the soul must be "essentially realized in some matter or other." Thus, it is a principle of the *DA* that whatever psychology investigates, even the faculty of thought, must be essentially realized in matter since psychology is part of physics.

That Aristotle is committed to the contention that every part of the soul, even voῦς, must be essentially enmattered is not as evident in *Meta* 6.1 as Wedin would have one believe. All that T4 requires for a certain soul being considered by a student of nature is that that soul not be without matter; it does not require that the soul be essentially realized in some matter or other. If there were a kind of soul that were completely without matter, this would not be investigated by physics. Thus, T4 seems to preclude the sort of strong separation that would make of the soul or one of its parts a separate substance. On the other hand, T4 seems to fall well short of requiring that the physicist study only souls whose every act is essentially realized in matter. If there were a kind of soul, some of whose acts were not realized in any material part, but whose other acts were, then such a soul would fit the *Metaphysics*' requirement that it be "not without matter." Granted, this is not the obvious suggestion of T4, but the passage is at least open to this sort of strong separation. Its very openness seems to speak against Wedin's claim that essential material realization is required for all of the soul's parts to belong to the physical science of psychology. Thus, on the basis of *Meta* 6.1, the physical investigation of soul in the *DA* may yet include a soul or power of soul that is separate$_s$.

When Wedin turns to the *DA*, he sees Aristotle's discussion of the method appropriate to the investigation of the soul as prescriptive and carrying the implication that all faculties of soul are enmattered. He notes that *DA* 1.1 explicitly includes the study of the soul within physics, and that this inclusion shapes Aristotle's whole approach to the subject.[31] It is in this spirit that Wedin cites Aristotle's claim that even thinking is dependent on imagination. Since imagination for Aristotle is a sense power that requires a bodily organ, Wedin thinks voῦς, too, is tied to the body. As Aristotle says:

T5: In most cases none of the affections, whether active or passive, exist apart from the body. This applies to anger, courage, desire and sensation generally, though possibly thinking is an exception. But if this too is a kind of imagination, or at least is not without imagination, even this cannot exist without the body. If then any function or affection of the soul is peculiar to it, it will be separate from the body; but if there is nothing peculiar to the soul it will not be separate. . . . For it is not separate, if it is always associated with some body. It seems these affections of the soul are associated with the body—anger, gentleness, fear, pity, courage and joy, as well as loving and hating; for when they appear the body is also affected. (403a6–13, 15–19)[32]

Wedin reads this passage first as asserting the strict requirements for the soul or one of its parts to be separate$_S$, and second as claiming that νοῦς does not in fact meet these requirements. "A property will be peculiar to the soul if and only if it applies to the soul and to the soul only. If at least one property is peculiar, then it is possible for the soul to be separated."[33] For νοῦς to be separate$_S$, then, it can neither be, nor depend on, anything physical. "So the question is whether there are any essentially mental or nonphysical predicates, that is, predicates whose subjects neither are nor depend on entities, states or processes that themselves take physical predicates."[34] But, if thought is dependent on imagination, then it will not be peculiar to the soul alone: "even it will depend on the body should thought turn out to involve images."[35] This fact, then, violates what Wedin considers to be a condition for strong separation. Thus, Wedin sees Aristotle as claiming that if the soul were separate$_S$, an investigation of it would not be part of physics.[36] This passage, and the whole chapter from which it comes, *DA* 1.1, then, is Aristotle's insistence on the inclusion of matter in the explanation of soul and all of its parts, even the faculty of thought. As Deborah Modrak observes: "Aristotle makes psychology a part of physics and this, Wedin argues, reveals Aristotle's materialist stance."[37]

Understood this way, *T5* certainly precludes the possibility of including a Cartesian mind in Aristotelian physics. However, it precludes only this extreme kind of immaterial mind. On Wedin's reading, not only is a mind subject to physical predicates barred from strong separation, but it also is one that depends on what is so subject. Thus, Wedin believes that the very dependence of νοῦς on the bodily power of imagination ensures its inclusion within physics, which could only happen if the mind were itself a bodily power. Again, the possibility of another kind of strong separation that would qualify as not without matter (as in T4) seems to have escaped Wedin. Although T5 precludes νοῦς being a completely separate substance, it is possible that the activity of νοῦς is an affection peculiar to the soul alone while at the same time being dependent on imagination.

Wedin's approach seems to misconstrue Aristotle's pronouncement that the study of the soul is part of physics. Wedin seems to take this to be an *a priori* principle, such that whatever is studied in a science that Aristotle has declared to be physical, *ipso facto*, must explain its subject as an enmattered form. As Thomas Aquinas points out, however, the fact that the science of the soul is a part of physics is actually a *conclusion* from the fact that all, or a least most, affections of the soul also involve the body.[38] Noticing that the body is an integral component in seemingly all activities attributed to the soul, Aristotle concludes that the study of the soul ought to be conducted by the scientist who uses both form and matter in his explanations, that is, the physicist. This preliminary conclusion, however, is not an announcement that because the physicist studies the soul, all its faculties must therefore involve matter. Merely assigning the study of the soul to the physicist, then, should not be understood to signal Aristotle's denial that voῦς is separate$_S$. If voῦς were to turn out to be separate$_S$, it seems that it must be the physicist who determines that fact.

Aristotle's claims in *DA* 1.1 concerning the separation of voῦς, then, are more modest and more subtle than Wedin acknowledges. T5 asserts that its dependence on images implies that voῦς does not exist apart from the body. It asserts further that if a part of the soul has no function or affection peculiar to itself, then it is not separate$_S$ from the body. Given these two assertions, it would be a fallacy, however, to conclude that because voῦς depends on images, it has no function or affection peculiar to itself. Because a faculty that depends on images does not exist without the body and whatever is not peculiar to the soul alone is not separate$_S$ from the body, it does not follow that an activity that does depend on images, as thinking indisputably does, is not peculiar to the soul. What T5 notably does not say is that no part of the soul has an operation peculiar to it alone and that voῦς is not separate. T5 is thus compatible with an understanding of mind that is separate$_S$, yet dependent for its exercise on imagination, for example, to provide the content of its activity of thinking.

This passage from *DA* 1.1 seems to allow that the intellect may have an activity peculiar to itself, while nevertheless being dependent on images. Noῦς, then, may be separate$_S$ and so not be realized in any bodily structure; nevertheless, voῦς does depend on the body since it depends on imagination (432a6–8). This admission trades on a distinction that Wedin does not seem to recognize, the distinction between being dependent on the body and being realized in bodily structures. Modrak has noticed that this distinction lies behind the assertions that Aristotle makes in T5. "Aristotle is entitled to draw a distinction between being a capacity possessed by a body and being a capacity exercised through a body" (cf. 408b20–25).[39] For Wedin, Aristotle's claim that νοῦς is dependent on images, and so on the body in which images are realized, is tantamount to saying that νοῦς is realized in the body (bodily structures), just not in any one set of bodily structures. However, T5 seems to resist the conflation of bodily dependence with bodily realization by allowing that νοῦς has the former, but not the latter.

Thus, T5 seems to be opening up some logical space for a notion of separation that is neither unrelated to the body nor realized in it. It does so by allowing that the intellect may have affections peculiar to the soul, but because it is dependent on images, it does not occur apart from a certain kind of body. Furthermore, T5 places the study of such an intellect, which is separate$_s$, within the study of physics precisely because it is dependent on images.

Aristotle in this early part of the *DA* entertains three possibilities: (1) all affections belong to the soul alone[40]; (2) some affections do; or (3) none do. Functionalists, such as Wedin, are correct in asserting that Aristotle wishes to deny (1). However, the mere denial of (1) does not entail that (3) is true. Simply because it is not true that all affections belong to the soul alone, it does not follow that no affection belongs to the soul alone, as Wedin claims when he denies that νοῦς is separate$_s$. Moreover, the denial that all affections belong to the soul alone is sufficient for the investigation into such affections (which constitutes the bulk of the *De Anima*) to be a work of physics. The truth of the claims contrary to (1) (i.e., either that some affections or no affections belong to the soul alone) are to be determined in the *De Anima*.

Wedin's interpretation, moreover, would leave Aristotle with a curious incongruity. If it were true, as Wedin believes, that Aristotle wants an account of all psychic faculties that require mention of the body, then Aristotle seems surprisingly noncommital on the matter. The last lines of T5 (403a12–13) seem intended to open up the possibility that νοῦς is separate$_s$ from the body, but not to preclude the possibility: "If then any function or affection of the soul is peculiar to it, it will be separate from the body; but if there is nothing peculiar to the soul it will not be separate." If the line that preceded this one (403a11), which claims that the dependence of thinking on imagination implies that it cannot exist without the body, meant that a notion of νοῦς as separate$_s$ would not be part of Aristotle's concern in the *DA*, then there is no need for the antecedent of 403a12: "If then any function of the soul is peculiar to it." The possibility of the strong separation, then, is a theoretical option that Aristotle, at this point in the *DA*, wants to keep open.[41]

The fact that this passage from *DA* 1.1 (T5) is making room for a notion of the mind's strong separation indicates that Aristotle intended his later arguments in *DA* 3.4 and 3.5 to prove that νοῦς enjoys strong separation. Only if he were going to prove the strong separation of νοῦς in Book 3 would he need to unify the *DA* by integrating strong separation into his generally physical psychology in Book 1. Because Aristotle will come to the conclusion that νοῦς has an activity in which the body does not share, he does need to tie such a conclusion to the study of the other powers of the soul, powers that have no acts apart from bodily organs. Aristotle effects this connection with the rest of the study into affections of the soul that belong also to the body by his claim that νοῦς is dependent on imagination. Nevertheless, he allows the possibility that in spite of this dependence, νοῦς may still have an act peculiar to itself, apart from the body.

The Distinctiveness of Noῦς

Wedin claims that Aristotle believes that νοῦς, while having no simple realization, is nevertheless a material power. As evidence, he cites two passages where a nonstandard account of a faculty is said to be required for νοῦς.[42] In these citations, Wedin apparently only means to show that νοῦς has a different relationship to bodily structures than other cognitive faculties, but has an ultimately physical realization, nonetheless. On examining these passages, it seems clear that, whatever unique relation to the body he has in mind, Aristotle does not think that the nonstandardness of his account of νοῦς is the weak separation envisioned by Wedin. The first text Wedin cites is as follows:

T6: But in the case of the mind and the thinking faculty nothing is yet clear; it seems to be a distinct kind of soul, and it alone admits of being separated, as the eternal from the perishable. (*DA* 2.2, 413b24–27)

Wedin's cognitivistic account of νοῦς emerging from the cognitive processes and states that are directly realized in physical structures could hardly fit with T6. For although Wedin's account does require that νοῦς be separate in the weak sense, this weak sense would hardly count as something that "alone admits of being separated, as the eternal from the perishable." Wedin's point is just that νοῦς is perishable. Therefore, it is not separable from what is perishable in the same way that the eternal is.

While not so clearly at variance with his interpretation, given its context, Wedin's second citation certainly will not allow for the sort of weak separation that he has in mind either.

T7: For those perishable creatures which have reasoning power have all the other powers as well. But not all those that have any one of them have reasoning power; some have not even imagination, while others live by this alone. There is another account for speculative mind. (*DA* 2.3, 415a9–15)

At first blush, this passage might be thought to be compatible with Wedin's interpretation. However, noting the context, it seems to positively militate against his reading of the separability of νοῦς. For the context of T7 is that the different genera of faculties form a hierarchy: the sensitive faculty is always found with the vegetative, but the vegetative is separate from the sensitive in the sense that the former is found without the latter (415a1–3). Likewise, the rational is always found with the sensitive, but the sensitive is separable from the rational in the same way as the vegetative is from the sensitive. Given this notion of separability, the point of T7 seems to be that the higher faculties normally are not separable from the lower. Insofar as νοῦς is a higher faculty emerging from lower ones, as Wedin's interpretation would have it, it should not be separable in this sense. Thus, when Aristotle claims that the speculative faculty is another question, he seems to mean that it could exist apart from other psychic faculties, as, for example, the vegetative faculty does. However, being a higher faculty, this would go against the general rule just outlined. The point, then, of the difference in the separability enjoyed by νοῦς is just that it can exist without other powers of the soul, since this ability to exist apart is the only notion of separation that T7 considers.

Separation and the Actualities of the Body

Wedin claims in yet another note that his interpretation, which favors weak separation, is justified by claims made earlier in the *DA*. "Indeed, as the sense given to χωριστὸς (separate) at the outset of Aristotle's analysis (II.1, 413a3–7), it would appear to govern the discussion of separation in the balance of the work."[43] Again, when one turns to the passage in question, Aristotle seems to be noting just the possibility that Wedin would deny.

T8a: Just as the pupil and the faculty of seeing make an eye, so in the other case the soul and body make a living creature. It is quite clear, then, that neither the soul nor certain parts of it, if it has parts, is separate from the body; for in some cases the actuality belongs to the parts themselves. Yet truly, nothing prevents that this not be the case for some (parts of the soul) because they are not actualities of any body. (*DA* 2.1, 413a3–7)

T8b: Furthermore, it is unclear whether the soul is the actuality of the body as the sailor is of the ship. (413a7–9)[44]

It is generally true that the parts of the soul are the actuality of certain parts of the body, and so they only exist in such parts as their actuality. Likewise, the whole of the soul, as the actuality of the body, only exists in the body. If, however, some part of the soul was the actuality of no part of the body, this general rule would not obtain, and such a part would be separate from the body. Aristotle, however, admits that the soul may be related to the body as the sailor is to the ship.

If this is the notion of separation that is to govern the balance of the work, then clearly Aristotle is making allowances for strong separation. It is quite true that Aristotle does believe that sense faculties are the actuality of organs as the soul as a whole is the actuality of the body. It is for this reason that he denies that such faculties are separate. What is most relevant to the present discussion is the kind of separation Aristotle is denying. It is that sense faculties are separate from the body, and, without further specification, such separation seems strong. Moreover, after giving his definition of soul as "the first actuality of a natural body possessed of organs" (412b5), Aristotle claims that this should settle the question of whether body and soul are one; they shall be one as the wax and the impression it receives are one (412b4–8). Aristotle, then, is quite aware that there are dualists who would want to make of soul and body two things such that the soul is separate$_s$ from the body. In fact, however, soul is the first actuality of a natural body having organs with the potentiality for life. Together, soul and body make one living thing. According to his general notion of soul, which applies to plants, animals and humans (and without any qualifications to the contrary), soul cannot be separate$_S$ from the body of which it is the act any more than a part of the soul can be separate$_S$ from the part of the body of which it is the act. After making this general claim, however, he does offer a qualification to the contrary, namely, that a part of the soul that is not the actuality of any body may be separate. In this qualification, Aristotle clearly means to allow that some part of the soul may be separate$_S$, since this is the only sense of separate he has entertained.

Wedin takes up separately the analogy between the soul and the sailor in T8b as something that the proponents of strong separation consider to be particularly strong evidence in favor of their interpretation. He reads the analogy as suggesting that the soul is the efficient cause of the body's movement, based on the use of the same analogy by Aristotle in the *Physics* and elsewhere in the *De Anima*. In particular, Aristotle says that the soul moves itself incidentally, as an oarsman moves a boat (408a29–34). Wedin then concludes that this analogy has only slight application to the issue of the soul's separation, strong or weak.[45]

Wedin's easy dismissal of T8b ignores its context. It may be the case that Aristotle is alluding to the soul's capacity as an efficient cause, but given that T8b follows Aristotle's suggestion that some parts of the soul might not be the actuality of any body, the soul-body/sailor-ship analogy seems to further suggest that Aristotle has strong separation in mind. The separation that is enjoyed by what is not the actuality of any body certainly seems to count as strong. Granted that none of T8 is definitive, what it does suggest seems to undermine Wedin's denial of the strong separation of νοῦς. If T8 lays out the sense of separation that governs all discussions in Book 3 concerning the separation of νοῦς, then it certainly seems to require a notion of separation stronger than what Wedin suggests.

Mind as Unaffected

In a final attempt to discredit any interpretation of νοῦς that favors strong separation, Wedin claims that those passages that allegedly support this interpretation are amenable to his cognitivist interpretation. One of these (413a8–9), we have dealt with already when examining the passage in which it appears (T8). The other is as follows:

T9: Mind seems to come about as a sort of substance and [seems] not to be destroyed. For it would be destroyed by the feebleness of age, if by anything; but as things are, it is similar to the case of the sense organs. For if an old man acquired a certain sort of eye, he would see as well as a young man. Thus, old age is due to something having happened not to the soul but to what it is in as in drunkenness and disease. Thus thinking and contemplating decay because something else within is destroyed, but in themselves they are unaffected. But discursive thinking and loving and hating are not affections of this but of that individual which has it in so far as it has it. Hence, when this is destroyed there is neither memory nor love, for these did not belong to it but to the composite thing which has perished. Likewise, mind is something more divine and is unaffected. (*DA* 1.4, 408b19–30)[46]

Wedin notes that T9 asserts that both mind and what is perishable have a measure in the divine; since mind is more divine than the perishable, the perishable must be somewhat divine as well. Aristotle merely claims that mind has a greater share of divinity, but that this does not actually assert that mind is separate_s. Wedin believes that the point here is that all psychic activities are destroyed with the destruction of their subserving systems. Thinking and contemplating are likewise said to decay and perish, so that neither the initial denial that mind perished nor its being likened to the divine entail that it is somehow eternal. One cannot destroy the form or functional description directly, but only the structures that subserve the form or function, and this applies to both perceptual and noetic faculties. Thinking and contemplating are only different from perceiving and so forth, in being higher-level functions, and so further removed from direct physical realization.[47] Because thought relies on images, and images on bodily structures, destruction of the structures results in destruction of both images and thoughts. "Thus there is no suggestion in the passage that νοῦς is an intellectual substance that may exist without body."[48]

Obviously Aristotle, in T9, is claiming that there is a difference between bodily passions and mind, according to which each is said to decay. At 408b25–27, he is posing a contrast between certain passions, that is, discursive thinking (διανοεῖσθαι), loving and hating on the one hand, and thinking (νοεῖν) and contemplating (θεωρεῖν) on the other. The latter are unaffected in a way that the former are not. Thinking and contemplating are unaffected in their own right (b26); the passions are affections of the individual (b27) and belong to the composite (b29). As such, they would necessarily be bodily passions.[49] Thus, there seems to be a basic contrast between noetic activities and the passions that belong to a composite of body and soul.

What makes T9 so difficult is the obscurity of some of Aristotle's references. For example, he says that the passions are not affections of that (ἐκείνου) but of such a thing (τουδὶ) having that (ἐκεῖνο) insofar as it has that (ἣ ἐκεῖνο ἔχει). He seems to be saying that the named passions are not affections of mind (alone), since he just said that thinking and contemplating are in their own right unaffected. However, if this is what Aristotle intends, then he appears to be speaking a little imprecisely. For he seems to be saying that this, presumably the mind, is that in virtue of which an individual is an individual. Such a description suggests instead that the soul is the referent of ἐκεῖνο. If this is the case, then it seems that the soul, by which is probably meant the soul alone, is that of which the passions are not affections. Furthermore, since he is in the midst of contrasting noetic activities and passions, one can infer that noetic activities do belong to the soul alone. Given also that he has said that many, if not all, properties of the soul also belong to the body (*DA* 1.1), it is highly probable that Aristotle means that the passions are bodily, while noetic activity is not. If this were the case, thinking and contemplating would be unaffected, which in this context means unmovable, and so nonperishable. Since they belong to the soul alone, they only decay when something else within perishes. But διανοεῖσθαι, loving and hating, are not affections of the soul (alone); they belong to the individual, which is composed of body and soul.

When Wedin says that those cognitive functions that are the forms of their organs or bodily structures are not destroyed directly, he is correct. But, he overlooks the fact that T9 is making a distinction between the passions and νοῦς. On Wedin's interpretation, there is no very significant difference; his point is that both sense faculties and the mind are perishable. The only difference between the two sorts of capacities is that noetic activities are higher-order functions further removed from bodily structures. Since, however, Aristotle sees the difference in terms of whether or not the soul alone is the subject of these activities, it is wrong to think that all cognitive faculties are the forms of some bodily part or emerge from such forms.

When Aristotle continues in T9 by considering the ultimate fate of the passions, his contrast with noetic activities again indicates that the latter might enjoy strong separation. He says that when the individual is destroyed, there is neither memory nor love because memory and love belong to the individual composite, which is destroyed. Again, he says that they did not belong to that (ἐκεῖνο), which, allowing for some ambiguity, refers to either νοῦς or the soul alone. It is only after setting up this other contrast that Aristotle attributes greater divinity to νοῦς. The implication is that νοῦς enjoys a different fate than memory and love, and since these passions are fated to perish, one may reasonably suppose that νοῦς will not. Granted its tentative nature due to being in the dialectical first book of the *DA*, T9 still suggests strong separation in spite of Wedin's contrary interpretation.

T9 seems to be making the sort of subtle distinction seen earlier, and so it resists the blanket denial of strong separation that Wedin had alleged. Wedin might be right that the passage contains no suggestion that νοῦς is "an intellectual substance that may exist without the body." However, this does not necessarily defeat the claim that T9 endorses the strong separation of νοῦς, since, as has been repeatedly suggested, a substance capable of nonbodily existence is not the only sense of strong separation. Νοῦς is still separate$_s$ since its own proper act is not simultaneously the act of some part, or collection of parts, of the body. Thus, T9 still favors strong separation because it endorses the distinction drawn earlier between a faculty that depends on the body and a faculty that is realized in the body: νοῦς depends on the body but is not realized in the body. Evidence that Aristotle endorses this distinction is found in the fact that he claims that νοῦς does not perish (οὐ φθείρεσθαι) (408b20), even though thinking and contemplating decay because something within perishes (καὶ τὸ νοεῖν δὴ καὶ τὸ θεωρεῖν μαραίνεται ἄλλου τινὸς ἔσω φθειρομένου) (408b25). Thus, the claim in T9 that thinking decays when something within perishes mirrors the claim in T5 that, because thinking depends on imagination, it cannot exist without the body (403a8–10). Likewise, the claim in T9 that νοῦς does not perish and the implication that thinking belongs to the soul alone[50] mirror the claim in T5 that any activity that belongs to the soul alone can be separated (403a10–11). Thus, T9 supports the interpretation that Aristotle favors the strong separation of νοῦς, against the interpretation of Wedin.

CONCLUSION

Of all the texts that Wedin marshals in defense of his thesis that Aristotle's doctrine of νοῦς is materialist, an early version of cognitivism, none gives unequivocal support, while few give any support at all. Aristotle's attitude toward the separability of νοῦς in these texts falls into four basic categories. The texts from Book 3 (T1, T2 and T3) form one group and assign to νοῦς some manner of separation, but the character of this separation is precisely what is in dispute. Consequently, I shall not enlist them as support for either strong or weak separation. Of Aristotle's three remaining groups of texts, the first does give some qualified support to Wedin's interpretation. For Wedin repeatedly insists that, according to Aristotle, the intellect is not a separate intellectual substance (or an immaterial Cartesian mind). Accordingly, *Meta* 6.1 (T4) and *DA* 1.1 (T5) clearly do indicate that Aristotle believes that neither the soul nor any of its parts is a substance distinct from the body. However, in another category of texts, Aristotle speculates that νοῦς has a relation to the body unlike other parts of the soul, a relation inconsistent with Wedin's interpretation. Aristotle suspects that νοῦς alone is separable as an immortal thing (T6), that it might be a power capable of existing without the sensitive or vegetative powers (T7), and that it is something more divine that does not perish but only decays when something else perishes (T9). Aristotle's elaborations on the distinct nature of the relation of νοῦς to the body comprise the last category of texts. In these, Aristotle claims that νοῦς is separate because its acts are peculiar to the soul (T5), not the actuality of any body (T8), and do not belong to the individual, composed of soul and body, but to the soul alone, that is, that in virtue of which the individual is what it is (T9). Given the weight of this evidence, it seems that Aristotle does believe that νοῦς is separate from the body in a strong sense, thus defeating Wedin's materialist interpretation.

NOTES

1. Howard Robinson, "Aristotelian Dualism," in *Oxford Studies in Ancient Philosophy*, vol. 1 (Oxford: Oxford University Press, 1983); see also Howard Robinson, "Mind and Body in Aristotle," *Classical Quarterly* 28 (1978): 105–124; Robert Heinaman, "Aristotle and the Mind-body Problem," *Phronesis* 35, no. 1 (1990).

2. K. V. Wilkes, *Physicalism* (Atlanta Highlands, NJ: Humanities Press, 1978).

3. K. V. Wilkes, "*Psuchē* versus the Mind," in *Essays on Aristotle's* De Anima, ed. Martha C. Nussbaum and Amélie Oksenberg Rorty (Oxford: Clarendon Press, 1992).

4. Deborah Modrak, "The *Nous*-body Problem in Aristotle," *Review of Metaphysics* 44, no. 4 (1991): 757.

5. Michael V. Wedin, *Mind and Imagination in Aristotle* (New Haven: Yale University Press, 1988).

6. Ibid., pp. 160–161.

7. Robinson, "Mind and Body in Aristotle," pp. 124–128.

8. Modrak, "The *Nous*-body Problem," p. 757.

9. Wedin, *Mind and Imagination*, p. 160.

10. Ibid., p. 116.

11. Ibid., p. 165.

12. Throughout this chapter, significant texts of Aristotle will be labeled T1, T2 and so forth in order to facilitate references in the text.

13. ἀνάγκη ἄρα, ἐπεὶ πάντα νοεῖ, ἀμιγῆ εἶναι ὥσπερ φησὶν Ἀναξαγόρας, ἵνα κρατῇ, τοῦτο δ᾽ ἐστὶν ἵνα γνωρίζῃ· ;παρεμφαινόμενον γὰρ κωλύει τὸ ἀλλότρτον καὶ ἀντιφράττει, ὥστε μεδ ἀυτοῦ εἶναι φύσιν μηδεμίαν ἀλλ᾽ ἢ ταύτην, ὅτι δυνατός.

14. ὁ ἄρα καλούμενος τῆς ψυχῆς νοῦς (λέγω δὲ νοῦν ᾧ διανοεῖται καὶ ὑπολαμβάνει ἡ ψυχή) οὐθέν ἐστιν ἐνεργείᾳ τῶν ὄντων πρὶν νοεῖν. διὸ οὐδὲ μεμῖχθαι εὔλογον αὐτὸν τῇ σώματι· ποιός τις γὰρ ἂν γίγνοιτο, ἢ ψυχρὸς ἢ θερμός, ἢ κἂν ὄργανόν τι εἴη, ὥσπερ τῷ αἰσθητικῷ· νῦν δ᾽ οὐθέν ἐστιν.

15. Wedin, *Mind and Imagination*, p. 164; see also ibid., p. 166.

16. Ibid., p. 58.

17. ἐπεὶ δὲ περὶ φαντασίας ἐν τοῖς περὶ ψυχῆς εἴρεται, καὶ ἔστι μὲν τὸ αὐτὸ τῷ αἰσθητικῷ τὸ φανταστικόν, τὸ δ᾽ εἶναι φανταστικῷ καὶ αἰσθητικῷ ἕτερον . . . φανερὸν ὅτι τοῦ αἰσθητικοῦ μέν ἐστι τὸ ἐνυπνιάζειν, τούτου δ᾽ ἡ τὸ φανταστικόν.

Ibid. Wedin notes on page 51 that in this passage nothing more is implied than that the same thing is both what perceives and what has imagination. As he explains, the thing engaging in both activities is the perceiving subject, that is, animal having both faculties. Indeed, he denies that Aristotle is claiming that both functions belong to the same faculty, considered from two different perspectives. The context of this passage for *On Dreams* (*Ins*), however, is Aristotle's attempt to assign dreaming to a particular cognitive faculty. If the only criterion for that assignation were that the thing that dreams also engage in some other cognitive activity, then each faculty, even those excluded by Aristotle (δοξα or νοῦς ἡ[459a8]), would qualify as the faculty of dreaming. Wedin, then, undercuts Aristotle's whole basis for identifying the φανταστικόν with the αισθητικόν.

18. καὶ οὗτος ὁ νοῦς χωριστὸς καὶ ἀπαθὴς καὶ ἀμιγής τῇ οὐσίᾳ ὢν ἐνεργείᾳ.

19. Wedin, *Mind and Imagination*, p. 182. In fairness to Wedin, he also cites other texts from Book 2 of the *De Anima* to support the weak separation of

νοῦς. They are 2.1, 413a3–7; 2.2, 413b24–27; and 2.3, 415a11–13. These texts are discussed as T8, T6 and T7 respectively.

20. χωρισθεὶς δ' ἐστὶ μόνον τοῦθο ὅπερ ἐστί, καὶ τοῦτο μόνον ἀθάνατον καὶ ἀΐδιον.

21. Wedin, *Mind and Imagination*, p. 190.

22. Ibid., p. 192.

23. *APr* 1.31, 46b3–17; *APo* 2.5, 92a1–2; *Top* 2.3, 110a37–b4; *Top* 3.6, 119b35–37; *Top* 4.2, 122b37–123a10; *Top* 5.1, 128b19–20; *NE* 10.8, 1177b32–38.

24. *Top* 4.2, 122b12–17; *Top* 6.6, 145b21–33.

25. *Phys* 3.4, 203b3–15; *Phys* 8.1, 250b10–14.

26. *De Caelo* 1.3, 270b1–11; *De Caelo* 2.1, 283b26–284a11.

27. *APo* 1.24, 84b16–22; *NE* 6.2, 1139b19–35.

28. Wedin, *Mind and Imagination*, p. 6.

29. Ibid.

30. καὶ διότι καὶ περὶ ψυχῆς ἐνίας θεωρῆσαι τοῦ φυσικοῦ, ὅση μὴ ἄνευ τῆς ὕλης ἐστίν.

31. Wedin, *Mind and Imagination*, p. 7.

32. φαίνεται δὲ τῶν μὲν πλείστων οὐθὲν ἄνευ τοῦ σώματος πάσχειν οὐδὲ ποιεῖν, οἷον ὀργίζεσθαι, θαρρεῖν, ἐπιθυμεῖν, ὅλως αἰσθάνεσθαι. μάλιστα δο ἔοικεν ἴδιῳ τὸ νοεῖν· εἰ δ' ἐστὶ καὶ τοῦτο φαντασία τις ἢ μὴ ἄνευ φαντασίας, οὐκ ἐνδέχοιτ' ἂν οὐδὲ τοῦτ' ἄνευ σώματος εἶναι. εἰ μὲν οὖν ἔστι τι τῶν τῆς ψυχῆς ἔργων ἢ παθημάτων ἴδιον, ἐνδέχοιτ' ἂν αὐτὴν χωρίζεσθαι· εἰ δὲ μηθέν ἐστιν ἴδιον αὐτῆς, οὐκ ἂν εἴη χωριστή. . . . ἀχώριστον γάρ, εἴπερ ἀεὶ μετὰ σώματός τινός ἐστιν. ἔοικε δὲ καὶ τὰ τῆς ψυχῆς παθήματα εἶναι μετὰ σώματος, θυμός, πραότης, φόβος, ἔλεος, θάρσος, ἔτι χαρὰ καὶ τὸ φιλεῖν τε καὶ μισεῖν· ἅμα γὰρ τούτοις πάσχει τι τὸ σῶμα.

I have followed Janonne's edition (*Aristote De l'âme*, ed. A. Jannone and E. Barbotin [Paris: Budé, 1966]) for line 19, which reads παθήματα for πάθη πάντα in W. D. Ross, ed., *Aristotle De Anima* (Oxford: Clarendon Press, 1961), lifting the restriction that *all* of the affections of the soul occur with the body. This is supported by the omission of any rational activity from the list of affections that follows.

33. Wedin, *Mind and Imagination*, p. 7.

34. Ibid.

35. Ibid.; see also p. 247.

36. Ibid.

37. Deborah Modrak, "Aristotle, the First Cognitivist?" *Apeiron* 23, no. 1 (1990): 66.

38. *Commentary on Aristotle's De Anima*, Bk. I, lect. 2, n. 23.

39. Modrak, "The *Nous*-body Problem," pp. 759–760.

40. It should be noted that this present passage is not the only time Aristotle considers the possibility that some properties belong to soul alone: "some (essential attributes) seem to be affections peculiar to soul and others seem to belong to living things also, by virtue of the soul" (*DA* 1.1, 402a10).

41. See also *DA* 2.1, 413a7: "Yet some (parts of the soul) may be separated because they are not the actualities of any body." The passage from which this comes is discussed as T8a.

42. Wedin, *Mind and Imagination*, p. 165.

43. Ibid., p. 182.

44. ἔτι δὲ ἄδηλον εἰ οὕτως ἐντελέχια τοῦ σώματος ἡ ψυχὴ ὥσπερ πλωτὴρ πλοίου.

Ross's edition adds ἤ before ὥσπερ πλωτὴρ πλοίου; the passage would thus read, "it is unclear whether the soul is the actuality of the body *or* (if it is) as the sailor (is) of the ship (italics mine)". Such a statement would make it easier to claim that Aristotle seriously considers the possibility of the strong separation of either whole or part of the soul for it implies that being an actuality of the body is distinct from being like the sailor of a ship. Without the inclusion of ἤ in the text, one has the difficult task of deciding how a sailor is himself the actuality of a ship, and how Aristotle intends this to apply to the relation between body and soul. Unfortunately, this inclusion derives only from paraphrases of the *DA* by Philoponus and Themistius. It seems best to retain the reading of the text that derives from all the extant (complete) manuscripts.

45. Wedin, *Mind and Imagination*, pp. 214–216.

46. Ὁ δὲ νοῦς ἔοικεν ἐγγίνεσθαι οὐσία τις οὖσα, καὶ οὐ φθείρεσθαι. μάλιστα γὰρ ἐφθείρετ᾽ ἂν ὑπὸ τῆς ἐν τῷ γήρᾳ ἀμαυρώσεως, νῦν δ᾽ ἴσως ὅπερ ἐπὶ τῶν αἰσθητηρίων συμβαίνει· εἰ γὰρ λάβοι ὁ πρεσβύτης ὄμμα τοιονδί, βλέποι ἂν ὥσπερ καὶ ὁ νέος. ὥστε τὸ γῆρας οὐ τῷ τὴν ψυχήν τι πεπονθέναι, ἀλλ᾽ ἐν ᾧ, καθάπερ ἐν μέθαις καὶ νόσοις. καὶ τὸ νοεῖν δὴ καὶ τὸ θεωρεῖν μαραίνεται ἄλλου τινὸς ἔσω φθειρομένου, αὐτὸ δὲ ἀπαθές ἐστιν. τὸ δὲ διανοεῖσθαι καὶ φιλεῖν ἢ μισεῖν οὐκ ἔστιν ἐκείνου πάθη, ἀλλὰ τουδὶ τοῦ ἔχοντος ἐκεῖνο, ᾗ ἐκεῖνο ἔχει. διὸ καὶ τούτου φθειρομένου οὔτε μνημονεύει οὔτε φιλεῖ· οὐ γὰρ ἐκείνου ἦν, ἀλλὰ τοῦ κοινοῦ, ὃ ἀπόλωλεν· ὁ δὲ νοῦς ἴσως θειότερόν τι καὶ ἀπαθές ἐστιν.

47. Wedin, *Mind and Imagination*, p. 213.

48. Ibid., p. 214.

49. Cf. *DA* 1.1.

50. Cf. T8.

CHAPTER 3

The Similarities between Νοῦς and Sense

INTRODUCTION

Given that it is Aristotle's intention in *DA* 3.4 to show that the intellect (νοῦς) acts autonomously from the body, it is reasonable to consider whether the chapter's arguments are successful. The structure of the arguments, however, requires that we examine one more point as preliminary to the arguments themselves. It seems that Aristotle offers three arguments for the conclusion that the intellect is a non-bodily power, a conclusion he signifies by the terms "unmixed" (ἀμιγῆ—429a18), "not mixed with the body" (οὐδὲ μεμῖχθαι . . . τῷ σώματι—429a24), "apart from the body and separate" (ἄνευ σώματος . . . χωριστός—429b5) and "separate from matter" (χωριστὰ . . . τῆς ὕλης–429b23). All three of the chapter's arguments are based on a comparison between sense and intellect. Aristotle claims that the intellect and the senses, as cognitive powers, have a generic similarity. However, the fact that νοῦς differs from sense in an aspect that for the senses is associated with their organs indicates that νοῦς is not associated with any part of the body. Since all of the arguments of the chapter depend on it, the nature of the similarity between sense and intellect should be clarified before an evaluation of those arguments begins.

With a view to the conclusion that he will draw and the arguments by which he will draw it, Aristotle begins *DA* 3.4 by comparing νοῦς and sense.

If thinking is like perceiving, it must be either a process of being acted upon by what is knowable, or something else of a similar kind. Although impassive, this part, then, must be receptive of the form of the object and be potentially such as its object, although not identical with it: as that which can sense is to the sensible, so must mind be to the knowable. (429a13–18)

Given what he is intending to prove (that voῦς is a non-bodily power) and the manner in which he is going to prove it (voῦς can do what the senses are prevented from doing because of their organs), Aristotle explicitly claims that sense and voῦς are analogous, "as the sensitive is to the sensible, so must mind be to the thinkable" (429b18). Moreover, he specifies three ways that mind is like sense: as acted upon by its object (or something of a similar kind), as receptive (though impassive) and as potentially the same as its object. These three aspects will serve as the basis for each of the three arguments that he presents in *DA* 3.4.

Since Aristotle will use dissimilarities within these common features of sense and intellect to indicate that voῦς is non-bodily, not only do these common features need to apply to both powers, but they must also be realized in the organs of sense. For instance, if both the sense and intellect are receptive, the receptivity of sense must involve its organs so that what is different in the receptivity of voῦς implies that it has no organ.

Richard Sorabji, however, claims that those features that are common to Aristotle's accounts of sense and intellect are not features that apply to sense organs.[1] Sorabji further states that the points of similarity that Aristotle lists at the beginning of *DA* 3.4 are not part of his considered position concerning voῦς. Instead these features apply only to sensation and only to the process that the sense organ undergoes. Thus, for example, although in sensation there is the reception of form, such reception only occurs in the organ. Interestingly, all three aspects according to which Aristotle asserts that voῦς is analogous to sense are aspects that, according to Sorabji, form a group of features that are not used by Aristotle to describe any aspect of sensation other than the process that sense organs undergo when an animal sees red or feels heat.

Before we can judge whether Aristotle is successful in his efforts to prove that voῦς is a nonbodily power, therefore, we must first decide whether the analogy applies in the way that the arguments require. For if Sorabji is right and reception of form, as well as other notions, applies only to the physiology of sensation, then Aristotle's arguments in *DA* 3.4

cannot possibly succeed. Accordingly, we will first examine if the formulae that Sorabji says have exclusively physiological applications are used to refer to voῦς, a power without a physiological component. To this end, we will consult primarily *DA* 3.4 and *Meta* 12. Then, we will examine whether Aristotle's account of sensation requires that these formulae have an application beyond physiology, and what that application is.

"IF THINKING IS LIKE PERCEIVING . . ."

In his essay, "Intentionality and Physiological Processes," Richard Sorabji claims that Aristotle maintains a sharp distinction between the formal and material causes of sensation.[2] Consistent with this claim, Sorabji interprets a cluster of Aristotelian formulae about sensation as descriptions that exclusively pertain to perception's material cause. This material cause, according to Sorabji, is the process that the sense organ undergoes during an episode of sensation. These Aristotelian formulae fall roughly into three main groups: the claim that what perceives receives form (which I will call the formal reception thesis), the claim that what perceives receives form without matter (which I will call the anahylic reception thesis[3]), and the claim that what perceives becomes actually "like" or "such" as its object, from being potentially "like" or "such" as its object (which I will call the likeness thesis). According to Sorabji, when Aristotle asserts any of these three theses, he is referring to one and the same physiological process by which the organ becomes *actually and literally* black or white, hot or cold, dry or moist.

This physiological account, however, is not Aristotle's only explanation of sensation. Sorabji tells us that Aristotle does have another doctrine concerning the sense power becoming *aware* of its object, but it is expressed in the quite different terms of "actual identity." In *DA* 3.2 (425b26–426a26), Aristotle explains sense perception in terms of his general theory of causation in *Physics* 3.3, where actual teaching and actual learning are said not to constitute two activities, but one and the same activity that goes on in the learner. "The application to sense perception of this causal theory is that the activity of a sound in working on one's hearing and the activity of hearing are not two activities, but one and the same activity, and [are] located not in the organ but in the sense (en tēi kata dunamin)."[4] Sorabji, however, immediately makes the point that "this doctrine about the activity of *sense* tells us nothing about whether the *organ* takes on sound."[5]

It becomes aware by becoming the object perceived

Sorabji notes that two of what he says are purely physiological descriptions, that is, the formal reception thesis and the likeness thesis, are linked "at 429a15–16, where it is said that if thinking is like perceiving, the thinking part of the soul must be able to receive form and be potentially such as its object."[6] Although this passage is part of Book 3, Chapter 4, of the *De Anima*, a chapter devoted to explaining how the faculty of thought, νοῦς or mind, is separate from the body, Sorabji claims that these descriptions apply to nothing other than the physiological aspect of sensation. They are merely the beginning of Aristotle's treatment of νοῦς, "the first tentative comparison"[7] with sensation according to a physiological description, but a comparison he soon abandons. Although Aristotle does say that νοῦς possesses forms (e.g., in thinking of a stone [431b28–432a1]), according to Sorabji, νοῦς does not receive such forms, much less are they received without matter.

The stone is not described as "matter" and its form is not spoken of as "received," probably because these words have expressed a doctrine about the sense-*organ*, and thinking does not in the same way involve an organ, in his view. Instead, the comparison is with the doctrine which does not concern the organ but the sense, that the activity of sound is in the sense and is not merely such as, but identical with, the activity of hearing.[8]

For Sorabji, then, the faculties of sense and of thought, on the one hand, and the organs of sense, on the other, cannot be described in the same terms. The formal reception thesis and the anahylic reception thesis cannot apply to νοῦς since they only apply to organs, and νοῦς has no organ. On the other hand, although the faculty of thought, like the sense faculty, does become one with its object, it does not do so, however, by receiving the form of its object. What does receive form, that is, the sense organ, merely becomes *such as*, but not identical with, its object. At least part of Sorabji's claim that expressions describe the physiological processes of sensation but have no application beyond the physiological, then, requires that Aristotle does not describe νοῦς in the same terms. If either the formal reception thesis, the anahylic reception thesis or the likeness thesis applies to νοῦς, then that fact would undermine Sorabji's claim that these descriptions apply exclusively to sense organs.

I believe, however, that Sorabji is mistaken about Aristotle's description of νοῦς. Even after the introductory remarks about the similarity between sensation and thought, Aristotle, in his considered position in

DA 3.4, continues to maintain that the faculty of thought *receives* its objects. While it is not as obviously asserted as the thesis that the objects of thought are without matter (430a3–6; 431b28–432a1), nevertheless, the formal reception thesis clearly applies to the activity of νοῦς, since it provides a key to the first main argument of the chapter. Moreover, νοῦς, like sense, passes from potential to actual conformity with its object. While such conformity is explicitly expressed in terms of identity, it is nevertheless equivalent to the power becoming such as its object is actually and thus like its object. All these descriptions (formal reception, anahylic reception, likeness and identity) apply to νοῦς throughout *DA* 3.4. Coupled with what he says in the *Meta*, Aristotle's account of νοῦς, then, is remarkably unified and incorporates just the Aristotelian formulae that Sorabji claims apply only to sensation, and only to sensation's material cause. Because these descriptions apply to a faculty that Sorabji admits has no organ, he cannot maintain his restriction of the formal reception thesis to the sense organs alone.

RECEPTIVITY IN *DA* 3.4

Although he does not engage in an extended exegesis of *DA* 3.4, analysis of this chapter, from which Sorabji draws his example of the coupling of the formal reception principle and the likeness principle, shows that νοῦς is indeed receptive. While many translations of this chapter do not make the receptive nature of νοῦς obvious, other translators and commentators clearly do consider this fact to be so obvious as to be unremarkable. Charles Kahn, for instance, simply translates a key passage of this chapter as though the intellect's receptivity were completely uncontroversial:

The intellect, since it thinks all things, must be unmixed (with any) . . . for (if it were mixed with some feature, that feature) would intrude and obstruct and hinder (the reception of) what is alien to it; hence *nous* has no nature other than this: the capacity (to receive noetic form).[9]

However, since there is disagreement among scholars as to whether νοῦς receives forms, the point deserves some analysis and justification.

In analyzing this chapter, one first finds Aristotle arguing throughout that νοῦς is in some significant way non-bodily. Aristotle in this chapter seems to give three main arguments for this thesis. First, however, he proposes the comparison between thinking and perceiving, the comparison that Sorabji calls "tentative" and one that Aristotle later abandons. Aristotle tells us that "if thinking is like perceiving, it must be either a process of being acted upon by what is knowable or something else of a similar kind" (429a12) and goes on to say that the part of the soul by which it thinks "although impassive, then, must be receptive of the form of an object" (429a15). As a consequence of being like perceiving, thought is a "being acted upon" by its objects in some sense, and this implies that it, like sense, is still impassive and "receptive of form." Aristotle can maintain that νοῦς, like sense, is both a "being acted upon" and "impassive," since, as he explained in 2.5, the "being acted upon" that characterizes sense is a special kind that should receive a special name (417b12–17). It is this distinct aspect of sense that merits the label "impassive," and this distinct aspect applies to νοῦς as well. If the comparison with sensation as receptive of form is merely tentative, as it is on Sorabji's interpretation, the point of the comparison, then, seems only to show that νοῦς is impassive in a manner similar to the sense faculty.

What follows this comparison is the first of the three arguments that say that νοῦς enjoys a special kind of separateness from the body. Aristotle argues that νοῦς is "unmixed," based on the fact that its range is limitless. For this argument to succeed, however, it is necessary that νοῦς receive its objects.

It is necessary then that the mind, since it thinks all things, should be "unmixed" (ἀμιγῆ), as Anaxagoras says, in order that it may be "in control," that is, that it may know. For the intrusion of anything foreign hinders and obstructs it. Hence the mind, too, can have no characteristic except its capacity to receive (429a18–22)[10]

Aristotle apparently believes that, given that the intellect has all things for its objects, it is necessarily unmixed with any of them. However, if one supposes, as Sorabji does, that being an object of the intellect has nothing to do with the intellect receiving it as an object, then Aristotle's support for this claim seems baffling. Aristotle's next line apparently makes the counter-factual claim that, if the intellect had anything foreign intruding, it would be hindered and obstructed, which apparently we are to believe is not the case (429a20). Hence, the sense of "hinder" and "obstruct" conveyed here is that of short-circuiting, that is, the simple nonfunctioning of the intellect. The principle seems to say that if the intellect had a foreign nature intruding upon it, then it would just not work at all.

Reading 429a20 this way, it seems to be a rather perplexing statement. What makes it so perplexing is the phrase "the intrusion of anything foreign." One could understand more easily how the intrusion of something foreign could be a hindrance if Aristotle were talking about an organ of a knowing power, for example, the eye. A mote of dust could be in the eye, and this could hinder its performance. However, Aristotle evidently is talking about a power that has no organ (429a26). The intellect, precisely because it has no organ, cannot have something foreign present, in the sense of intruding from an extrinsic source, and yet be hindered. For if something is present to this non-bodily power, then either it is constitutive of itself (in which case it is not foreign), or it is the intellect's object (in which case the intellect is not hindered). However, one and the same thing cannot be both foreign to the intellect and a hindrance to its operation. If the intrusion of something foreign that hinders the intellect is an impossible situation, then it is utterly mysterious why Aristotle should say that it is the reason why the intellect, which knows all, is unmixed.

The fact that 429a20 does not seem to make much sense in itself is our first indication that something is wrong. D. W. Hamlyn interprets this argument of *DA* 3.4 (almost) exclusively in terms of the identity thesis whereby the intellect becomes its object. He, like Sorabji, sees Aristotle's formula about receiving form without matter as intelligible only with regard to sense organs.[11] Noting that 429a16 identifies two formulae as points of similarity between sense and intellect (i.e., the formal reception thesis and the likeness thesis), he believes that the first is so tied to Aristotle's account of a physiological process in the sense organ that it is unintelligible when applied to νοῦς. Thus, he reads this argument for the intellect being unmixed as follows:

> The intellect must be unmixed with anything, since it thinks everything, and is thus, according to the formula, potentially like all things without being actually such. It must therefore be solely potential, if it is to think all things, and is before thinking nothing actual. If it contained anything actual it could not *become* this, as it must do according to the formula if it is to think it.[12]

Hence, for Hamlyn, the claim that the intellect is unmixed means that it is nothing actual. This conclusion follows from the two premises:

"whatever knows is potentially, but not actually like its object" and "the intellect knows all things."

This interpretation has a certain plausibility since it captures part of Aristotle's thought on knowing powers. However, two points speak against it being Aristotle's whole intent. First, it does not really take into account 429a20, which I have tried to show is troubling and needs explaining. According to Hamlyn, the line merely asserts that the intellect, in order to become like its object, cannot already be actually like its object. Second, Hamlyn's construal makes Aristotle's point that the intellect is nothing actual before it thinks to be just a repetition of the claim that the intellect is unmixed. For Hamlyn, this is not surprising since he reads the separation and unmixed character of the intellect in the weakest way possible.[13] However, for Aristotle, the fact that the intellect is nothing actual until it thinks is some further point beyond the point that it is unmixed. This is why he introduces the point as a *conclusion.*[14]

An examination of the overall structure of Aristotle's argument shows the inadequacy of this reading of the text. The argument consists of two universal premises and a universal conclusion. The first premise is as follows:

1. Whatever foreign nature that is present to a power, hinders (i.e., prevents the operation of) that power.

The conclusion claims:

3. The intellect is unmixed.

If we assume that "unmixed" is equivalent to "does not have a foreign nature present," it is clear that the only hope Aristotle has for making a valid syllogism is to claim as the minor premise:

2. No intellect is hindered.[15]

However, there are still two problems with the argument as thus presented. First, what is the justification for the major premise; why should "the intrusion of anything foreign" entail being hindered? Second, although all he would have to assert as evidence for the claim that νοῦς is not hindered is that the intellect actually knows something, Aristotle's actual minor premise is "νοῦς knows all things." The argument, then, seems to require a stronger connection between something not being present when the intellect knows all things and the implication that the intellect is unmixed.

Only if we posit that νοῦς is receptive of its objects can we make sense of the connection Aristotle sees between the universal capacity of νοῦς and its status as unmixed. Aristotle's logic requires that he connect the intellect with being unmixed by a denial that it is hindered, which he seems to think he accomplishes by claiming that νοῦς knows all things. Only on the supposition that knowledge is a kind of reception would it be necessary for Aristotle to claim that νοῦς knows all things in order to deny that it is hindered. Given this supposition, however, if the intellect were to know less than all things, it would be hindered from receiving some objects, and so be restricted in some way. Any other sense of knowledge, for example, the knower simply becoming identical with the object (without receiving it), could take place without necessarily being a knowledge of all things, and still the knowing power would not be hindered. Thus, the only way Aristotle's actual words can measure up to the demands of his argument is if knowing is a kind of receiving. Consequently, the claim that "νοῦς knows all" has to be equivalent to "νοῦς receives all." This is also equivalent to the claim that there is nothing that νοῦς does not receive, that is, νοῦς is not hindered. "To hinder," then, as Aristotle is using the term, does not mean "fails to function" as Hett's translation would lead one to believe, but rather means "impedes or blocks the reception of something."

Understanding Aristotle's use of "hinder" in this sense gives the necessary justification for the connection between knowing all things and being unmixed. The universal scope of νοῦς implies that it lacks the hindrance that it would have if something were present, only because νοῦς receives what it knows and is *thereby* united with its object. Thus, because there is in fact no restriction on what νοῦς receives, Aristotle concludes that νοῦς does not have the hindrance of something being present and, as it were, displacing its object. For Aristotle, it is in virtue of the intellect's receptivity that there is an implied equation between having nothing present and being unmixed, an equation that does not apply to the senses. For although the senses are relatively unhindered, the fact that they do not receive all forms, that is, know all things, but only the forms of their proper objects, is to be explained by the fact that they are mixed, that is, that they have organs.

Aristotle's connection between the intellect's universal receptivity and its having nothing present also causes his other conclusion, that is, that νοῦς has no nature other than to be in potency prior to knowing (429a22–24), to make sense. The intellect has no nature beyond its receptive capacity, since such a nature would prevent the reception of some form (and so it would not receive them all). Instead, it is merely possible to receive its objects and to be united with them, since to receive a form is the same as to be united with its object. Both of these points deserve a fuller elaboration. For the present, however, we can conclude that on the force of the logic of the argument, νοῦς is indeed receptive of form.

Given that Sorabji is highly critical of the ancient and medieval commentary tradition on other interpretive points, it is not surprising that we find a member of that tradition, Aquinas, disagreeing with him on his understanding of νοῦς. Aquinas took 429a20 to mean that the presence of some nature in a knowing faculty hindered that faculty in receiving that nature. As he says in his commentary on the *De Anima*, "Anything that is in potency with respect to an object, and able to receive it into itself, is, as such, without that object."[16] The intellect, however, is unrestricted with respect to what it can know, for it can know all things, and so in itself it lacks all of the natures that it receives. "If the intellect were restricted to any particular nature, this connatural restriction would prevent it from knowing other natures."[17] Thus, according to Aquinas's interpretation, since the intellect receives the forms of all bodies, it must lack the form of any body. Aquinas, therefore, concludes that the intellect is spatially separate, that is, it has an operation in which the body does not share. Even though Aristotle's version of the argument does not claim that the intellect knows all *bodies*, Aquinas's interpretation nevertheless accords with the overall structure of Aristotle's argument by understanding the intellect to be receptive.

The interpretation of νοῦς as receptive gains further support if one examines the Greek. In Greek, 429a20 reads: παρεμφαινόμενον γὰρ κωλύει τὸ ἀλλότριον καὶ ἀντιφράττει. What is essential for Aquinas's interpretation is that τὸ ἀλλότριον be translated as the object of κωλύει and ἀντιφράττει, as the translation of William of Moerbeke, from which Aquinas worked, renders the passage: "For what appeared inwardly would prevent and impede what was without."[18] In this translation, "what was without" (*extranem*) is William's rendering of τὸἀλλότριον, and in Latin it is clearly the direct object of "prevent and impede" (*prohibebit et obstruet*), William's rendering of κωλύει and ἀντιφράττει respectively.[19] It seems that Aquinas's reading, prompted by William's translation, then, fits more with the thrust of Aristotle's argument, since "hinder" in the argument carries with it the notion of blocking the reception of something. For, only if νοῦς is receptive is Aristotle's claim that νοῦς knows all things evidence that the intellect is unimpeded with respect to what it receives (τὸ ἀλλότριον). The reading that Aquinas and William give the passage highlights the fact that Aristotle has not changed his mind with regard to the claim at 429a15 that thinking, like sensation, involves the reception of form.

In addition to the added coherence that it gives to the argument of *DA* 3.4, there is other evidence that Aristotle meant ἀντιφράττει to convey the sense of impeding the reception of something with τὸ ἀλλότριον as its object. Of the six other genuine uses of ἀντιφράττειν in Aristotle's work, as opposed to those in works of questionable authenticity, four of them concern something (the earth or some celestial body) blocking the light of the sun or the moon in an eclipse, but all of them require that the word mean "block the passage or reception of something."[20] A typical example can be found at *Posterior Analytics* 2.2 (90a18) where Aristotle explains that in an eclipse, the earth hinders the light of the moon. "What is an eclipse? The privation of the moon's light by the interposition of the earth."[21] In this passage, Aristotle clearly uses ἀντιφράττειν to signify that something blocks or stands in the way of moonlight. In this context, the verb does not, nor could it, mean simply "to prevent the operation of something," as Hett's reading of 429a20 would require. Since Aristotle uses the verb ἀντιφράττειν to describe the obstruction and nonreception of an object of observation elsewhere, it lends further support to the reading of 429a20 given by William Moerbeke and interpreted by Aquinas where τὸ ἀλλότριον is the object of ἀντιφράττει, and what appears inwardly (παρεμφαινόμενον) is not something foreign.

Given my reconstruction of his argument, I hope it is apparent that, for Aristotle, the faculty of thought is legitimately characterized as being receptive of its objects. To construe Aristotle as holding that it is not renders a significant part of *DA* 3.4 to be of highly questionable internal coherence, since it makes it seem that he is claiming that something foreign might intrude into a power that has no organ and render that power inoperable. Moreover, failure to acknowledge the intellect's receptivity renders what is clearly supposed to be an explanation (mind is unmixed because it knows all things) otiose and virtually unrelated to the logic of his argument. Finally, the denial of the claim that νοῦς is receptive forces onto Aristotle's Greek a sense that is inconsistent with other uses of the same words. For these reasons, it seems best to hold that, at least through his first argument in *DA* 3.4, Aristotle did not begin his treatment of νοῦς with a merely tentative comparison between the faculties of thought and perception according to the formal reception thesis, only to later abandon the claim that this thesis holds for νοῦς. Rather, throughout this part of the chapter, Aristotle believes that νοῦς is receptive since its receptivity is essential for the validity of his argument and the consistency of his thought.

Νοῦς IN *METAPHYSICS* 12

Contrary to the view that the formal reception thesis was abandoned by Aristotle after this first argument in *DA* 3.4 that νοῦς is unmixed, in the *Meta* Aristotle also holds that νοῦς is receptive. In the *Meta*, however, one need not engage in a prolonged analysis of the argument and its various interpretations to show this, since Aristotle explicitly claims that νοῦς is receptive. In his attempt to explain how the first mover can be completely actual, Aristotle likens God to what in our experience is most actual, that is, theoretical thought. Thus, God is entirely intellectual activity, such that not even the fact that thought is directed toward an object reduces his actuality. As he explains this total unified actuality, Aristotle appeals to a general characteristic of the more familiar case of human thinking. In the process, he gives us confirmation that the intellect does indeed receive its object, and that it thereby becomes one with what it thinks.

And thought thinks itself through participation in the object of thought by the act of apprehension and thinking, so that thought and the object of thought are the same, because that which is *receptive* of the object of thought, i.e., essence, is thought (italics mine). (*Meta* 12.7, 1072b20–23)[22]

It is clear from this passage that for Aristotle thought becomes one with its object by receiving that object. Thus, he links the identity thesis with the reception of the object of thought. While Aristotle does not explicitly assert the formal reception thesis, he nevertheless describes its object as essence (οὐσία), and essence in its most proper sense is form.[23] Also, as Sorabji points out, in the *DA* Aristotle is explicit that the object of the intellect is indeed form (431b28–432a1). Thus, this text from the *Meta* shows us that the intellect receives that form, a point that Sorabji denies.

In the *Meta* there is also confirmation that this reception is anahylic. Again, discussing how God can be identified with his activity of thought, Aristotle explains that the intellect only becomes identified with its object because its object is without matter. Aristotle connects the identity principle with the claim that its objects are without matter by explaining the former by means of the latter.

[I]n some cases the knowledge is the object. In the productive sciences, if we disregard the matter, the substance, i.e., the essence, is the object; but in the speculative sciences the formula or the act of thinking is the object. Therefore since thought and the object of thought are not different in the case of things which contain no matter, they will be the same, and the act of thinking will be one with the object of thought. (*Meta* 12.9, 1074b36–1075a5)[24]

Deborah Modrak notes that, although both the acts of sensation and the acts of thinking are identical with their objects, the identity thesis applies more strongly to νοῦς, "namely, when the object is one of the things without matter, an abstract universal, an object of theoretical science (1075a3–5), for then the object of the cognitive activity is itself a thought."[25]

Three points about Aristotle's doctrine of νοῦς emerge from these two passages of the *Meta*. First, the intellect "receives" its object, and thereby becomes one with it (1072b20–23)—that is, the identity thesis applies to νοῦς because the faculty of thought is receptive. Second, the object of the intellect is essence, for which Aristotle uses the technical vocabulary οὐσία (1072b20–23) and τὸ τί ἦν εἶναι (1074b37). Third, the intellect becomes one with its objects insofar as these objects are without matter (1074b36–1075a5).

There is no doubt that two of these three characterizations of νοῦς in the *Meta* are paralleled in the *DA* account of νοῦς; I have tried to argue that the other one, the first in the following list, is also expressed in the *DA*. First, as the previous analysis shows, the intellect receives its objects (429a18–22). Aristotle, however, is just as explicit in the *DA* as in the *Meta* in describing the object of the intellect as essence (τὸ τί ἦν

εἶναι) (429b20). Likewise, Aristotle uses parallel expressions in both the
DA and the Meta to claim the object of thought, the νοητόν, is without
matter; in the DA it is said to be separate from matter (χωριστὰ τὰ
πράγματα τῆς ὕλης) (429b23), while in the Meta it is said to be without matter (ἄνευ ὕλης ἡ οὐσία καὶ τὸ τί ἦν εἶναι, 1075a2; μὴ ὕλην
ἔχει) (1075a4). Furthermore, Aristotle asserts this link between the
identity thesis and the object of thought being without matter in words
similar to the Metaphysics' description in DA 3.4: "For in the case of
things without matter, that which thinks and that which is thought are
the same; for speculative knowledge is the same as its object" (430a3–
6).[26]

LIKENESS AND IDENTITY

So far, one can see that the formal reception thesis, the anahylic thesis
and the identity thesis all apply to Aristotle's treatment of νοῦς. The
question of whether the likeness thesis applies as well is as yet unan-
swered. This is the most important question since Sorabji grants that
the identity thesis is non-physiological, and while he believes formal
reception and anahylic reception are physiological, he allows that they
may not be. Sorabji is adamant, however, in his belief that Aristotle
claims that only sense organs pass from potential likeness to actual
likeness.

In the latter part of DA 3.4, however, Aristotle implicitly claims that
both the identity thesis and the likeness thesis apply to νοῦς; he thereby
signals that the two principles are not distinct in his theory. At 429b30,
Aristotle proposes the identity thesis as an answer to a possible problem
that he sees in his treatment of νοῦς. The question asks: "if mind is
simple and impassible and has nothing in common with anything else
as Anaxagoras says, how can it come to think at all, given that thinking
is a passive affection?" Thus, the problem for Aristotle's account of νοῦς
as unmixed and separate is that thinking nevertheless still seems to be
a kind of being acted upon. This was one of the bases for the claim that
νοῦς and perception are analogous (429a13); it provides further evidence against the contention that the first comparison was merely tentative but later abandoned. As a kind of passive affection, νοῦς would
seem to need to have something in common with what acts upon it,
since acting and being acted upon, in the ordinary senses of those terms,

takes place in virtue of something common to both. For this reason, he tells us that the answer to this problem is the same as to a related problem:

> Or there is the explanation which we have given before of the phrase "being acted upon in virtue of something common" (πάσχειν κατὰ κοινόν), that mind is potentially identical with the objects of thought but is actually nothing until it thinks. (429b30–33)[27]

The identity thesis, then, is the same answer to the question of how what is affected is like what affects it.

Examining Aristotle's previous treatment of this problem, one finds that the identity thesis was not the answer he gave before, at least not explicitly. In Book 1, Chapter 5, Aristotle takes up for the first time in the *De Anima* the view that cognition requires something being common to both knower and known. He reports that some have supposed that the soul is "composed of the elements" in order "to account for the soul's perception and cognition of everything that is" (409b23–27). These thinkers believe that perception can only take place if what perceives is similar to the object perceived. On this view, perception is thought to be a kind of alteration, a kind of physical motion, and as such, the patient must have some nature in common with the agent in order to be affected by it. As Charlotte Witt notes, "And indeed the theory of perception, based on the principle that 'like is known by like,' which Aristotle criticizes, is one which analyzes perception in terms of a chain of motions between the object and the soul."[28]

If the soul already is or has the elements of which everything is made, it will already have the conditions necessary for the possibility of knowing anything and everything. As Aristotle relates, this theory's "supporters assume that like is known by like, as though they thus identified the soul with the things it knows" (409b25–28). For instance, in order to know things belonging to categories other than substance, the soul would have to have the elements of these other categories. The theory, however, fails as an explanation of such knowledge since there are no elements common to all the categories, much less any that the soul could have in common with what is in each of the categories (410a12–23). In 1.5, Aristotle disposes of this literal interpretation of the claim that the soul has "passions," that is, that it, undergoes motion and alteration in psychological processes, by pointing out this theory's shortcomings. As Witt explains,

For Aristotle, the central difficulty with this view is that it tries to explain how perception of everything is possible by holding that both soul and world are made up of the same material stuffs. But this fact, even if it were true, would not explain how we can perceive objects which are something over and above their material constituents.[29]

Thus, the theory that "like is known by like" assumes that cognition is a kind of motion or alteration and that agent and patient share something in common. So, when Aristotle criticizes this theory, he is criticizing the theory that cognition occurs because the knower is moved by having something in common with what it knows. In *DA* 1.5, he raises problems with considering cognition to be a case of "being acted upon in virtue of something common"; it is the same issue as claiming that like is known by like.

When Aristotle begins his own treatment of perception, he starts by tentatively accepting this theory, which he criticized in Book 1. He tells us that perception is an alteration and that like is in some sense affected (and thus known) by like.

Sensation consists in being moved and acted upon, as has been said; for it is held to be a sort of alteration. Now some say that like is affected only by like. But the sense in which this is possible or impossible we have already stated in our general account of acting and being acted upon. (416b33–417a3)[30]

This general account of acting and being acted upon refers to (GC) 1.7 and his claim that agent and patient are in a sense similar, and in a sense dissimilar, before any change.

But since only those things which either involve a "contrariety" or are "contraries"—and not any things selected at random—are such as to suffer action and to act, agent and patient must be "like" (i.e., identical) in kind and yet "unlike" (i.e., contrary) in species. . . . Hence agent and patient must be in one sense identical, but in another sense other than (i.e., "unlike") one another. . . . [P]atient and agent are generically identical (i.e., like) but specifically "unlike". (323b30–34; 324a4–6)[31]

He accepts this account of change in *DA* 2.5 and says that it applies to sensation. "Therefore, a thing is acted upon in one sense by like, in another sense by unlike, as we have said; for while it is being acted upon it is unlike, but when the action is complete, it is like" (417a19–21). The fact that the contexts of these two passages are in response to the same problem[32] confirms that it is this part of the *GC* that he has in mind. It is interesting to note that in *GC*, Aristotle uses the expression of likeness and identity interchangeably (ταὐτὰ καὶ ὅμοια) (324a6). Therefore, the mere fact that Aristotle uses "such" or "like" in the *DA* is not necessarily a sign that he is distinguishing this from identity. However, at this point in *DA* 2.5, he has not yet articulated the likeness thesis, that is, that what senses is potentially such as its object is actually and comes to be like it actually.

Aristotle then develops his account of sensation according to his principles of the potential and the actual into what we have been calling the likeness thesis. He distinguishes the kind of action that sensation is from ordinary alterations in which there is a destruction of the opposite quality (417b2ff.). The fact that there is no destruction of the opposite quality implies that the activity of sensation is not the imperfect action of an alteration, but the perfect activity of actuality in the second sense, "the realization of its nature" (417b16). It is only after distinguishing the activity of sensation from alterations that Aristotle proposes the likeness thesis:

The sentient subject is potentially such as the object of sense is actually, as we have said. Thus, it is acted upon while being unlike, but after having been acted upon, it has become like that object, and shares its quality. (418a3–6)

Thus, not only does he reject a straightforward application of "like is known by like," he also rejects a straightforward application of the notion that sensation is a material alteration.[33] What he does endorse is the view that sensation is *similar* to alteration, but instead of passing from a state of being merely unlike to a later state of being like (417a19–21), Aristotle's considered opinion is that the sensor is potentially like and becomes actually like the sense object.

The likeness thesis, then, is Aristotle's answer to the question of whether like is known by like. Thus, he is apparently referring to this discussion in *DA* 2.5 as "the explanation we have given before of the phrase 'being acted upon in virtue of something common'" (429b30–33). Although in *DA* 1.5 he considered what is wrong with the theory that like is known by like, in 2.5 he tells us what is right. Earlier he poses the problem of πάσχειν κατὰ κοινόν; here he gives his answer.

The development of this part of Aristotle's psychological theory shows that likeness and identity do not have two different applications within that theory, one to a material account, the other to a formal account. In Book 1, he claims that "like is known by like," as a theory that the soul suffers "passions" by having something in common with its objects, does not fully explain the facts. In 2.5 he says that perceiving is still a special sort of being acted upon, and so in a sense like is known by like. What knows is potentially like its object before perceiving, and actually like it after (418a3–6). Consequently, when Aristotle in *DA* 3.4 asks how thinking, whose faculty is simple and impassive and has nothing in common with its objects, can come about since thinking is a kind of being acted upon, he is clearly revisiting the "like is known by like" theory with respect to the intellect. He sees this theory of his predecessors as a case of being acted upon in virtue of something common (πάσχειν κατὰ κοινόν) and says the explanation that he gave before applies here too. He then cites the identity thesis. But if this is supposed to be the same answer he gave to the problem of like known by like, and that answer in 2.5 is the likeness thesis, then the likeness thesis *is* the identity thesis.

Thus, against the interpretation of Sorabji, when Aristotle says that what senses passes from potential to actual likeness and what knows passes from potential identity to actual identity, he is not stating two different theses about knowing, but one and the same thesis. For a knowing power to become actually like its object is for it to become one with it in actuality. Thus, in the case of sense, as Sorabji points out, Aristotle even there asserts that the sense power becomes one with its object. However, Aristotle does not use this description of what happens to the sense power to distinguish it from what happens to the sense organ. For Aristotle, when what senses (organ and power together) becomes such or like its object, it (the organ and the sense) is thereby becoming one, and also receiving the sensible form, and receiving this without matter.

CONCLUSION

From the foregoing consideration, it should be clear that Sorabji is incorrect in his contention that Aristotle does not describe νοῦς in terms that apply also to sensation, even as sensation occurs in sense organs. In addition to the similarity between sensation and thought that Aristotle asserts at the beginning of *DA* 3.4, throughout this chapter, as well as in *Meta* 12, he ascribes to νοῦς those features that Sorabji claims are characteristic of the operation of the senses in their organs. Thus, not only is the receptivity of νοῦς implied in the first argument—that it is unmixed (based on the fact that νοῦς has nothing appearing inwardly)—but it is also explicitly stated in *Meta* 12.7. In this latter passage, νοῦς is also said to become identical with its objects, that is, the essences or forms of things. Furthermore, in the latter part of *DA* 3.4, Aristotle implicitly identifies the claim that νοῦς becomes identical with its objects with the claim that it becomes like or assimilated to them. He does so by the fact that they are both offered as his explanation of how things are affected by what is common. Aristotle thus describes both νοῦς and the senses according to the same formulae (i.e., formal reception, anahylic reception, likeness and identity), both throughout *DA* 3.4 and in the *Meta*. In so doing, he applies to both cognitive faculties those formulae (anahylic reception and likeness) that Sorabji claims apply only to sensation, and only to sensation's material cause. Given, however, that Aristotle apparently is hoping to show that νοῦς acts apart from the body, the fact that all of these formulae apply to both may appear to endorse the view that what is proper to sensation is nothing physical, that is, nothing that really takes place in the sense organs.

NOTES

1. M. F. Burnyeat, "Is an Aristotelian Philosophy of Mind Still Credible? A Draft," in *Essays on Aristotle's* De Anima, ed. Martha C. Nussbaum and Amélie Oksenberg Rorty (Oxford: Clarendon Press, 1992), p. 23). Burnyeat sees Sorabji's account as supporting the interpretation of Aristotle as a functionalist. Indeed, S. Marc Cohen declares that Sorabji's interpretation "is one that a functionalist interpreter would find congenial" in his "Hylomorphism and Functionalism," in *Essays on Aristotle's* De Anima, ed. Martha C. Nussbaum and Amélie Oksenberg Rorty (Oxford: Clarendon Press, 1992), p. 61.

2. Richard Sorabji, "Intentionality, and Physiological Processes: Aristotle's Theory of Sense Perception," in *Essays on Aristotle's* De Anima, ed. Martha C. Nussbaum and Amélie Oksenberg Rorty (Oxford: Clarendon Press, 1992), pp. 211–212.

3. I use the term "anahylic reception" instead of other terms that suggest themselves (e.g., immaterial reception of form) to avoid the connotation of a theory about awareness or intentionality that Sorabji adamantly denies is Aristotle's. See Richard Sorabji, "From Aristotle to Brentano: The Development of the Concept of Intentionality," in *Festschrift for A. C. Lloyd: On the Aristotelian Tradition*, ed. H. Blumenthal and H. Robinson, supp. vol. (Oxford: Oxford University Press, 1991).

4. Sorabji, "Intentionality," p. 213.

5. Ibid.

6. Ibid., p. 212.

7. Ibid., p. 213.

8. Ibid.

9. Charles H. Kahn, "Aristotle on Thinking," in *Essays on Aristotle's De Anima*, ed. Martha C. Nussbaum and Amélie Oksenberg Rorty (Oxford: Clarendon Press, 1992), p. 376.

10. Aristotle, *On the Soul*, tr. W. S. Hett, Loeb Classical Library (Cambridge, MA: Harvard University Press, 1986), p. 165. ἀνάγκη ἄρα, ἐπεὶ πάντα νοεῖ, ἀμιγῆ εἶναι, ὥσπερ φησὶν Ἀναξαγόρας, ἵνα κρατῇ, τοῦτο δ᾽ ἐστὶν ἵνα γνωρίζῃ· παρεμφαινόμενον γὰρ κωλύει τὸ ἀλλότριον καὶ ἀντιφράττει · ὥστε μηδ᾽ αὐτοῦ εἶναι φύσιν μηδεμίαν ἀλλ᾽ ἢ ταύτην, ὅτι δυνατός.

11. Aristotle, *Aristotle's De Anima. Books II and III*, tr. D. W. Hamlyn, translation and commentary (Oxford: Clarendon Press, 1968), p. 136.

12. Ibid.

13. Ibid. "The intellect is distinct from the body in the way already suggested, that it is a potentiality and has no organ" (p. 137). "[T]he intellect is dependent for its existence on the senses" (p. 138).

14. "ὥστε μηδ᾽ αὐτοῦ εἶναι φύσιν μηδεμίαν ἀλλ᾽ ἢ ταύτην, ὅτι δυνατόν" (429a21). "διὸ οὐδὲ μεμῖχθαι εὔλογον αὐτὸν τῷ σώματι" (429a24).

15. Thus the argument is in the second figure, AEE:

$\forall x(Px \rightarrow Hx)$ All that has something present is hindered.

$\forall x(Ix \rightarrow \sim Hx)$ No intellect is hindered.

∴ $\forall x(Ix \rightarrow \sim Px)$ Therefore, no intellect has something present.

16. Thomas Aquinas, *Opera Omnia*, iussu Leonis XIII P. M. edita, Tomus XLV, *Sentencia Libri De Anima*, cura et studio Fratrum Predicatorum (Romae: Ex Typographia Polyglotta S. C. de Propoganda Fide, 1984), p. 203.

17. Ibid.

18. Ibid. Intus apperens enim prohibebit extranem, et obstruet.

19. In Hett's translation, τὸ ἀλλότριον modifies παρεμφαινόμενον; thus the phrase reads in English "the presence of *what is foreign to its nature*" (author's

emphasis). As far as I can tell, this reading is equally grammatical, but makes less sense given Aristotle's argument.

20. The four dealing with eclipses are *APo* 1.31, 87b40; *APo* 2.2, 90a18; *De Caelo* 2.13, 293b25; and *Meteor* 1.8, 345a29. The two others are *Meteor* 2.8, 368b10, and *De Juvent* 5, 470a13.

21. Aristotle, *Aristotle: Posterior Analytics*, tr. Hugh Tredennick, Loeb Classical Library (Cambridge, MA: Harvard University Press, 1984).

22. αὐτὸν δὲ νοεῖ ὁ νοῦς κατὰ μετάληψιν τοῦ νοητοῦ νοητὸς γὰρ γίγνεται θιγγάνων καὶ νοῶν, ὥστε ταὐτὸν νοῦς καὶ νοητόν. τὸ γὰρ δεκτικὸν τοῦ νοητοῦ καὶ τῆς οὐσίας νοῦς.

23. Meta 7.17, 1041b6–9; see also *DA* 2.1, 412b10–11.

24. ἢ ἐπ᾽ ἐνίων ἡ ἐπιστήμη τὸ πρᾶγμα, ἐπὶ μὲν τῶν ποιητικῶν ἄνευ ὕλης ἡ οὐσία καὶ τὸ τί ἦν εἶναι, ἐπὶ δὲ τῶν θεωρετικῶν ὁ λόγος τὸ πρᾶγμα καὶ ἡ νόησις; οὐχ ἑτέρου οὖν ὄντος τοῦ νοουμένου καὶ τοῦ νοῦ, ὅσα μὴ ὕλην ἔχει, τὸ αὐτὸ ἔσται, καὶ ἡ νόησις τῷ νοουμένῳ μία.

25. Deborah Modrak, "The *Nous*-body Problem in Aristotle," *Review of Metaphysics* 44, no. 4 (1990–1991): 755–774.

26. ἐπὶ μὲν γὰρ τῶν ἄνευ ὕλης τὸ αὐτό ἐστι τὸ νοοῦν καὶ τὸ νοούμενον.

27. ἢ τὸ μὲν πάσχειν κατὰ κοινόν τι διήρηται πρότερον, ὅτι δυνάμει πώς ἐστι τα νοητὰ ὁ νοῦς, ἀλλ᾽ ἐντελεχείᾳ οὐδέν, πρὶν ἂν νοῇ.

28. Charlotte Witt, "Dialectic, Motion and Perception: *De Anima*, Book I," in *Essays on Aristotle's De Anima*, ed. Martha C. Nussbaum and Amélie Oksenberg Rorty (Oxford: Clarendon Press, 1992), p. 181.

29. Ibid., p. 182.

30. ἡ δ᾽ αἴσθησις ἐν τῷ κινεῖσθαί τε καὶ πάσχειν συμβαίνει, καθάπερ εἴρηται · δοκεῖ γὰρ ἀλλοίωσίς τις εἶναι. φασὶ δέ τινες καὶ τὸ ὅμοιον ὑπὸ τοῦ ὁμοίου πάσχειν. τοῦτο δὲ πῶς δυνατὸν ἢ ἀδύνατον, εἰρήκαμεν ἐν τοῖς καθόλου λόγοις περὶ τοῦ ποιεῖν καὶ πάσχειν.

31. ἀλλ᾽ ἐπεὶ οὖ τὸ τυχὸν πέφυκε πάσχειν καὶ ποιεῖν, ἀλλ᾽ ὅσα ἢ ἐναντία ἐστὶν ἢ ἐνατίωσιν ἔχει, ἀνάγκη καὶ τὸ ποιοῦν καὶ τὸ πάσχον τῷ γένει μὲν ὅμοιον εἶναι καὶ ταὐτό, τῷ δ᾽ εἴδει ἀνόμοιον καὶ ἐναντίον · ... ὥστ᾽ ἀνάγκη πῶς μὲν εἶναι ταὐτὰ τό τε ποιοῦν καὶ το πάσχον, πῶς δ᾽ ὅτερα καὶ ἀνόμοια ἀλλήλοις. ἐπεὶ δὲ καὶ τὸ πάσχον καὶ τὸ ποιοῦν τῷ μὲν γένει ταὐτὰ καὶ ὅμοια τῷ δ᾽ εἴδει ἀνόμοια, τοιαῦτα δὲ τἀναντία, φανερὸν ὅτι παθητικὰ καὶ ποιητικὰ ἀλλήλων ἐστὶ τά τ᾽ ἐναντία καὶ τὶ μεταξύ.

32. The problem Aristotle addresses in both works is if like acts on like, why do things not act on themselves (cf. 417a3–10 and 323b19–24).

33. Cf. *GC* 324b5ff.

CHAPTER 4

The Relationship of Sense Powers to Their Organs

INTRODUCTION

Aristotle's arguments in *DA* 3.4 that νοῦς acts apart from any bodily organ appeal to what he believes are differences between sense and intellect. The intellect is unmixed or separate because it knows all things, while the senses are presumably restricted to a determinate range of objects. The intellect is not dazzled, which it would be if it had an organ. The intellect knows the essences of things, which are different from individual things themselves; while the latter are known by sense powers owing to their organs, their essences are known in a way other than through an organ. Thus, in order to argue that νοῦς does not have an organ, those cognitive powers that do have organs (i.e., the senses) have to have certain characteristics that are lacking in νοῦς. Accordingly, even if we were successful in showing that Aristotle does want to prove that the intellect acts apart from the body, he cannot do so by arguing from the differences between sense and intellect, unless these two sorts of cognitive powers are similar in the relevant ways. It is clear, though, that Aristotle does regard the two powers as similar in their reception of form (without matter), becoming like their objects, and becoming the same as their objects. However, even if this were true, but the reception of form, assimilation and identification by the senses did not involve bodily organs to a significant degree, the fact that the intellect differs from sense will not bear on whether the intellect acts without an organ, and so acts separately from the body. Therefore, before examining the arguments for the mind's separation, we will examine the question of whether and to what extent the senses rely on, and are determined by, their organs and any physiological changes therein.

THE SPIRITUALIST-LITERALIST DEBATE

Miles Burnyeat has recently sparked a debate among Aristotelian scholars over the correct interpretation of Aristotle's teaching on the relationship between sense powers and their organs. He claims that for Aristotle, the processes that sense organs undergo are at most a necessary condition for perceptual awareness. "[T]he physical material of which Aristotelian sense-organs are made does not need to undergo any ordinary physical change to become aware of a colour or a smell."[1] Instead, an animal becomes perceptually aware by the direct affectation of its sense powers by sensible qualities. "[F]or Aristotle the 'causal' agent (if such it may be called) of the unordinary change which constitutes perceiving is the colour or the smell itself."[2] Perception per se comes about when a sensible object comes into contact with a sense faculty, but such contact is not brought about by the sense organ undergoing any kind of physical change. According to Burnyeat, in Aristotle's theory "no physiological change is needed for the eye or the organ of touch to become aware of the appropriate perceptual objects."[3]

Furthermore, Burnyeat implicates Aquinas in this anti-physiological reading of Aristotle. According to Burnyeat, although Aristotle's several descriptions of sensation seem like they refer to ordinary physical processes, they refer instead to the decidedly nonphysical activity of perception. "All of these physical seeming descriptions—the organ's becoming like the object, its being affected, acted on, or altered by sensible qualities, its taking on sensible form without the matter—all these are referring to what Aquinas calls a 'spiritual' change, a becoming aware of some sensible quality in the environment."[4] For Burnyeat, "Aquinas gives an excellent account" of what Aristotle means by receiving form without matter, and thus how the activity of sense differs from the changes that non-sentient things undergo in ordinary alterations, that is, by receiving form with matter, for example, in being heated. "It follows that receiving the warmth of a warm thing without its matter means becoming warm without really becoming warm; it means registering, noticing or perceiving the warmth without actually becoming warm."[5] Stephen Everson, in deference to the imputation of Aquinas, calls Burnyeat's interpretation a "spiritualist" reading.[6]

In opposition to Burnyeat's spiritualist interpretation, Everson proposes to defend a "literalist" interpretation. He, like Sorabji, believes that for Aristotle, when an animal perceives, the sense organ undergoes a normal physiological change, as would any inanimate matter of the same sort. So, when one sees, Aristotle would maintain that the eye, that is, the water in the eye or the eye-jelly, undergoes the same sorts of physical changes that water would undergo if it were not in the eye, and that this is the physiological basis for perception as awareness. Moreover, this physical change is characterized by the organ becoming literally such as the object is, colored in the case of the eye, warm or hard in the case of touch and so forth. "According to the literalist interpreter, when a sense organ is activated and perception occurs, the organ is altered so that it literally becomes like its (proper) object: it takes on the property of the sensible which affects it."[7] So, in opposition to the spiritualist interpretation, Everson insists that a change in the sense organ is both necessary and sufficient to bring about actual perception, and that this change is the same sort of physical process that occurs when inanimate things are altered so as to have the same quality for themselves as what alters them.

THE PHYSICAL NATURE OF PERCEPTION

The proponents of the literalist interpretation argue persuasively that, for Aristotle, perception necessarily has a physical aspect. Everson, for instance, points to what Aristotle has to say about the physical requirements for something to serve as a sense organ, as well as to the breakdowns in the perceptual process that result from this, perceptual blind spots and the impediment to perception posed by intense perceptibles. Because of the rationale that Aristotle employs in specifying in some detail the physical constitution that sense organs must have in order to function properly, that is, to be appropriately related to their proper objects, the literalists conclude that perception involves processes occurring in the organ, a conclusion that Burnyeat resists.

Literalists such as Everson find support for their position in Aristotle's claims that sense organs have to have a certain material constitution in order to be affected by their proper sensible qualities. For example, the organ of sight must be made of such material as to be affected by the object of sight (i.e., color). Since the transparent is what is affected by color (418a31–b2, b26–a1), Aristotle says that the eye is composed of water, which, like air, has the transparent in it but is more easily confined and condensed than air (*De Sensu* 2, 438a12–14). Everson concludes that this shows that the material constitution of the organ is determined by the need of the organ to be able to be affected by the proper sensible and be so assimilated.[8] Thus, implicit in this is Aristotle's belief that the proper sensibles do affect the organs of perceivers. For Everson, the spiritualists' denial that sense organs are affected by their proper sensibles leaves them with no motivation for Aristotle's insistence that sense organs have a particular type of material constitution.[9]

Everson believes that the clearest case of Aristotle advancing the claim that perception involves sense organs undergoing physical processes occurs in the case of touch.[10] The physical nature of perception, especially evident in touch, causes perceptual blind spots to occur. Aristotle observes that one cannot feel what is as hot or soft as oneself, and explains this by appealing to the fact that the physical qualities of the organ of touch prevent the perception of what is already like itself.

The organ for the perception of these [the differentiae of body] is that of touch—that part of the body in which primarily the sense of touch resides. This is that part which is potentially such as its object is actually; for perception is a form of being affected; so that that which makes something such as it itself actually is makes the other such because the other is already potentially such. That is why we do not perceive what is equally hot and cold or hard and soft, but only excesses, the sense being a sort of mean between the opposites that characterize the objects of perception. It is because of this that it discerns [κρίνει] the perceptible objects. For what is in the middle is such as to discern; for it becomes either extreme in relation to the other. (*DA* 2.11, 423b29–424a7)[11]

Because the sense organ must have the quality of the object to be perceived only potentially, when the organ already has that quality actually, it cannot perceive; there is a "blind spot" to what has the same temperature as the part of the skin one is trying to feel with. Everson says that, for Aristotle, because the organ of touch is made of earth, it will already actually have a certain temperature and texture. Therefore, it will not be able to be affected by an object with these same qualities, that is, not by something equally hot or cold, or hard or soft. Only what is excessively so relative to the organ of touch can affect the sense and so be perceived.[12] Everson concludes that this explanation would not succeed if the sensory apparatus did not take on the sensible qualities in the same sense as those qualities are in the object. Indeed, the fact that Aristotle says that the perception generally, and touch specifically, is a kind of being affected indicates for Everson that Aristotle believes that the process in the organ is straightforward alteration as described in *On Generation and Corruption* 1.7.[13] According to Everson, the organ undergoes the alteration Aristotle describes in *GC* as would any inanimate substance with similar matter.[14] He also believes that Aristotle endorses the view that the process in the sense organ is an alteration at the end of *DA* 2.5, a point that will be examined again later. Literalists can explain this insistence because sense organs are composed of the sort of matter that is generally affected by the proper objects of the senses.[15] If the spiritualists were right and no physical process were necessary, then blind spots would not occur; but because blind spots do occur, perception is a physical process.

Moreover, a second case of perceptual breakdown, insensitivity due to intense perceptibles, highlights Aristotle's commitment to the physicality of perception, which is the core of the literalist position. In order for intense perceptibles to impede perception or destroy organs, it is necessary that perceptibles act on the physical organ of the perceiver. In fact, Aristotle cites the fact that the senses are dazzled by intense objects as a necessary premise in his argument that νοῦς is separate from the body.

For the sense faculty is not able to sense after an excessive sensible object; e.g., of sound immediately after loud sound, and neither seeing nor smelling is possible just after strong colours and scents; but when the mind thinks the exceedingly knowable, it is not less able to think of slighter things, but even more able; for the faculty of sense is not apart from the body, whereas the mind is separate. (429a32–b6)

The fact that νοῦς is not dazzled by its objects when these are intense would show that it does not have an organ only if the dazzling of the senses by their intense objects occurred in their organs.

The seeing of brilliant sights may disturb the ability to see, but the thinking of brilliant thoughts only improves the mind's acuity. But there would be no need to deny mind a physical organ if he did not think that there was *some* physical manifestation to cognitive awareness. His reasoning seems to be that if mind did have a physical organ then the thinking of brilliant thoughts would have a disturbing effect on the ability to think. This reasoning only makes sense if Aristotle also thinks that the disturbing effect would be manifested by a change in the physical state of the organ.[16]

Clearly, then, the fact that Aristotle appeals to the deleterious effects of intense perceptibles on sense organs in the demonstration of the mind's separation from the body shows that he believes that perception has a physical nature. Indeed, his need to make such a claim is the very reason this issue is being addressed.

Not only do intense perceptibles dazzle perceivers by disrupting the organ, but they also can destroy the organ. According to Aristotle, the senses are a kind of "ratio" and potentiality of the organs (424a27). This ratio is that in virtue of which a given body is a sense organ, and thus by having the given ratio, the organ is the sort of thing that can be affected by the sense object. Insofar as the sense power is affected, it is affected as being in the organ, and so the sense power and organ are affected together. This being so, Aristotle can give an explanation for how intense objects destroy sense organs.

It is also clear from this why an excess of perceptual objects destroys the sense organs; for if the excitement of the sense organ is too strong, the ratio of its adjustment (which, as we saw, constitutes the sense) is destroyed; just as the adjustment of and pitch of a lyre is destroyed when the strings are struck hard. (*DA* 2.12, 424a29–34)

Aristotle says here that what intense sensibles destroy are organs, but his explanation shows that this happens because the sensible upsets the sense, that is, the ratio in the organ. Thus, it seems, to destroy the sense power, for example, the ability to see, is to destroy the organ, for example, an eye, since an eye without the ability to see is not really an eye, but an eye in name only. It is essential to Aristotle's account of this fact, however, that sense objects cause organs to undergo some physical process. When the sense object is of sufficient intensity, it destroys the sense by disrupting the ratio in the organ that constitutes the sense power, and to disrupt the ratio of the organ seems to mean the organ is affected.

After all, this disruption spells the end for the organ as an organ. In this, it is clear that perceptible objects affect perceivers by acting on the sense organs since intense perceptibles destroy their "ratio" and thereby destroy them. Thus, there must be some kind of process occurring in the organs that the sensible objects are causing.

John Sisko has shown that, for Aristotle, the phenomena of the senses being dazzled necessarily implies that sensation involves organs undergoing physical processes. According to Sisko, the only ways to resist the conclusion that the objects of sensation, that is, perceptible qualities themselves, destroy organs by causing a physical process in sense organs is to claim that the ill effects of such occurrences either are due to a concurrent material cause or occur only in the unusual case of intense perceptibles.[17] Both these options are blocked by other passages on such impediments to perception. In *DA* 3.13, Aristotle claims that intense objects of touch destroy not only this sense, but the whole animal as well. This, however, is not due to a concomitant physical force, which Aristotle credits elsewhere for causing physical effects (e.g., the air that accompanies thunder, and not the sound itself, splits wood [*DA* 2.12, 424b11–12]).

Other sensibles, such as colour, sound and smell, do not destroy the animal by excess but only the sense organs; except incidentally, as for instance when a thrust or blow is delivered at the same time as the sound, or when other things are set in motion by the objects of sight or smell, which destroy by contact. (435b7–12)

Normally, intense colors, sounds and smells destroy only their respective organs and not the whole animal, unless some physical cause accompanying the sensible kills the animal. In that case, the sensible qualities would be incidental causes of the animal's death. The sensible qualities themselves, however, do cause the organs to be destroyed. "In this passage Aristotle clearly refers to cases in which intense perceptibles destroy the organ without there being a concurrent material cause. Thus, he must think that intense perceptibles themselves cause the destruction of the respective organs."[18]

Nor is the effect of perceptible objects on material organs operative only among an abnormal class, the intense perceptible. Sisko also sites *De Generatione Animalium* for evidence that even normal perceptibles can dazzle, and so impede a sense organ; normal perceptibles do so when they are stronger than the things that one later perceives.[19] Thus, even normal perceptibles affect sense organs, for example, by overwhelming some eyes that "are too much moved by the light and by visible objects in respect of their liquidity as well as their transparency, (since) sight is the movement of this part in so far as it is transparent, not in so far as it is liquid."[20] For Aristotle, all vision comes about through what is transparent in the eye, that is, the liquid, being moved. Vision fails, and one is dazzled, when the transparent is overcome by an excess of movement from sensibles that are either intense absolutely or relative to other less intense ones.

> But if the eye is to see, it must neither not be moved at all nor yet more than in so far as it is transparent, for the stronger movement drives out the weaker. Hence it is that on changing from strong colours, or on going out of the sun into the dark, men cannot see, for the motion already existing in the eye, being strong, stops that from outside, and in general neither a strong nor a weak sight can see bright things because the liquid is acted upon and moved too much. (780a7–14)

When a person goes into relative dark from intense colors or sunlight, he or she takes with himself or herself the relatively violent motions that were caused from seeing things outside, which motion accounts for him or her inability to later see indoors. Consequently, all dazzling is explained in terms of the material process that the sense organs undergo due to the influence of relatively or absolutely intense objects.

> Thus it would seem that when Aristotle compares the destruction of the organ by intense perceptibles to the loss of harmony and pitch in a lyre by too violent plucking (*DA* II.12 424a28–32), he intends this to be a strong analogy; the plucking (whether mild or violent) causes material alteration in the lyre and perceptibles (whether normal or intense) cause material alteration in the organ.[21]

Aristotle, then, repeatedly insists that organs suffer damaging effects from intense perceptibles, and that the sense qualities themselves, that is, the proper objects of perception and not a concomitant physical force, damage them. It seems clear, then, that some physical process occurs in the sense organs when an animal perceives. However, those who are strongest in their insistence that perception at least requires there be some physical aspect to it, also insist that the physical processes that the sense organs undergo are what Aristotle calls by the technical term "alteration" (ἀλλοίωσις) in *GC*. However, the task of determining the kinds of processes that sense organs undergo by which sense powers are actualized and an animal is aware of a sensible object is, in fact, a more complicated matter in the thought of Aristotle, for there are several passages where Aristotle denies that perception is a case of sense organs being altered in the technical sense.[22] These passages are, in fact, those which Burnyeat appeals to in support of his spiritualist position. Moreover, while it seems clear that perception must involve physical organs, it is far from clear that organs are affected by undergoing ordinary alterations. In order, then, to understand the sense in which objects of perception affect sense organs, as well as the restriction that organs place on sense powers, the relation between sense powers and their organs needs to be better understood. Fortunately, Aristotle offers several illuminating discussions concerning what that relation is.

TWO KINDS OF ALTERATION

In *DA* 2.5, Aristotle distinguishes two kinds of alteration and seeks to specify the manner in which each is applicable to perception. He begins by saying that "sensation consists, as has been said, in being moved and acted upon; for it is held to be a sort of change of state" (416b34–35).[23] Next, he wonders why the senses do not perceive themselves since they perceive other things made of the elements and they themselves are so composed (417a1–7) and concludes that perception, in itself, is a certain potency, and so is like the combustible that requires an external agent to make it burn (417a7–10). As a potency, it is present both when being exercised and when it is not (417a10–14). As there are two senses of "potential," so there are two senses of "actual": something which is able to acquire a potency to act is said to become actual in one sense when it acquires this potency, but when it exercises the potency it is actual in a second, higher sense (417a22–b2). This is all by way of preparation for what is the core distinction:

Even the term "being acted upon" is not used in a single sense, but sometimes it means a kind of destruction of something by its contrary, and sometimes rather a preservation of that which is potential by something actual which is like it, as potency is related to actuality. For when the one merely possessing knowledge comes to exercise it, he is not being altered (for the development is into his real self or actuality), or else is a different kind of alteration. (417b2–8)[24]

He then discusses the inadequacy of describing the exercise of knowledge as an alteration or as a teaching, as well as the shortcomings of calling the learning process a case of being acted upon (417b8–14). He concludes his distinction by saying that "there are two senses of alteration, one a change to a negative condition, and the other a change to a positive state, that is, a realization of its nature" (417b15–17). Everson labels these two senses of alteration "alteration₁" and "alteration₂," and explains the basic distinction between them: "When something undergoes alteration₁, it loses the property it had before the alteration and acquires a 'contrary' property; in alteration₂, it simply exercises a capacity it already possesses."[25] Although he does not elaborate on the correspondence, Everson does acknowledge that this distinction between two sorts of alteration corresponds to Aristotle's distinction between motion (κίνησις) and activity (ἐνέργεια) in *Metaphysics* 9.6 and *Nicomachean Ethics* 10.4.[26] While alteration₁ is clearly a physical process, alteration₂, in being distinct, might seem to be nonphysical. Aristotle identifies the act of perception with alteration₂ for he says, "Again, actual sensation corresponds to the exercise of knowledge" (417b19)[27]; as the exercise of knowledge comes about through an alteration₂ (417b7–8), so does actual perception. In *Meta*, he also identifies seeing with activity (1048b18–34). Everson, then, grants that *DA* 2.5 *appears* to support the spiritualist contention that the proper activity by which a perceiver is aware of its environment is not a physical process. The question for Everson is whether alteration₂ is the only sort of alteration operative in Aristotle's account of perception.

Everson, however, believes this chapter, in fact, supports the literalist interpretation, for he claims that the chapter shows that *both* kinds of alteration are involved in perception.[28] He says *DA* does not rule out alteration₁ applying to perception and that 2.5 never says that the change in the perceiver is "special."[29] However, if the spiritualist is to defend his or her contention that perception has no physical element, he or she needs

to show that the *only* alterations which the sense organs undergo are alterations₂. Again the argument of II.5 does not show this—only that they do undergo such alteration. It does not follow from this that no other kind of alteration is involved in perception—and there is nothing at all in II.5 to suggest that when perceptual alteration₂ does occur, this does not also require some more basic alteration₁ of the relevant sense organ.[30]

Granted that in perception there is an alteration₂, Everson believes the chapter does not preclude that an alteration₁, that is, a physical process, also occurs in the sense organ. Indeed, it seems he has good reason to think both kinds of alterations are operative.

Moreover, Everson claims that Aristotle in 2.5 positively endorses his claim that the organ undergoes alteration₁ since, without it, the spiritualist reading cannot accommodate the chapter's final lines. Aristotle concludes the chapter as follows: "The sentient subject is potentially such as the object of sense is actually, as we have said. Thus it is acted upon while being unlike, but after having been acted upon, it has become like that object, and shares its quality" (418a3–6). This is "something which the spiritualist cannot make sense of, since on that reading the organ would have to move from being perceptible to producing perception, rather than from being capable of perception to actually perceiving."[31] Apparently for Everson, since the spiritualist claims that the only way to characterize the perceptible object when actually being perceived is as producing perception, given that the perceiver becomes like this object in actuality, the perceiver becomes causative of perception since the object is also causative of perception.[32]

This objection to the spiritualist interpretation, however, seems misguided since not even the literalists could make sense of the passage in these terms. The sense of "like" Everson is employing in this objection is "like with respect to actuality," and not simply "like in quality." If this same sense of "like" were applied to his own understanding of the organ's assimilation to the object, the organ would pass from potentially affecting suitably situated perceivers, to actually affecting them. This may in fact be a consequence of his position, and as literally assimilated to their objects, sense organs will be perceptible in the same sense as their objects. However, even if he is comfortable with this sense of assimilation, it is surely secondary to the main claim that the organs come to have the quality in common.[33] The point of Aristotle's claim is that when assimilated to its object, the perceiver comes to have the same quality, and the spiritualist can maintain this claim by saying that what is assimilated comes to have that quality that the object causes it to have, without it thereby having the property of causing.

Aristotle insists that the sense *organs* must be potentially such as the sensible object is actually. This does not mean that the eye should actually be able to turn red. It need only imply that the eye takes on the same sensible form as is instantiated in the red rose and, at the higher level of activity, the same perceptible form might be manifested as an awareness of red. At this higher level of activity, the sensible form need not actually *be* red.[34]

Everson also claims that the beginning of the chapter supports the belief that there is an alteration₁ in perception. At 416b33–4 Aristotle says that "perception occurs in being changed and acted upon." According to Everson, if perception were only an alteration₂, Aristotle would have said that perception occurs in being acted upon; if only in alteration₁, he would have said in being changed. The fact that he says both indicates that both kinds of alteration are involved. Moreover, Everson believes that this line shows that in fact the being acted upon characteristic of alteration₂ exists *in* the change that is characteristic of alteration₁.[35] This line alone, however, is inconclusive for it is certainly possible that Aristotle means that both phrases describe a single process, that is, he may not mean to distinguish perception as a motion from perception as a being acted upon. Instead, he could merely be asserting that the one process is both of these things. Everson, then, needs more compelling evidence in order to secure his interpretation.

Everson appeals for support of his contention that perception involves both kinds of alteration occurring in the sense organs by citing *Physics* (*Phys*) 7.2. In this chapter, Aristotle is arguing that in all cases of motion, even alterations, mover and moved are in contact, and this principle applies even to the alterations undergone by perceivers.

Nor again is there anything intermediate between that which undergoes and that which causes alteration: this can be shown by induction; for in every case we find that the respective extremities of that which causes and that which undergoes alteration are together. . . . Thus we say that a thing is altered by becoming hot or sweet or thick or dry or white; and we make these assertions alike of what is inanimate and what is animate. And further, where animate things are in question, we make them both of the parts that have no power of perception and the senses themselves. For in a way the senses also undergo alteration, since actual perception is a change through the body, in the course of which the sense is affected in a certain way. Thus the animate is capable of every kind of alteration of which the inanimate is capable; but the inanimate is not capable of every kind of which the animate is capable, since it is not capable of alteration in respect of the senses. (244b1–2, 6–15)

Aristotle asserts that in perception there are two sorts of alteration, one of which both the animate and the inanimate are susceptible to, and another of which only the animate, that is the sensate, is capable. According to Everson, Aristotle is explicit in his contention that both animate and inanimate substances are capable of undergoing the alterations of becoming white, hot, sweet and so forth.[36] Aristotle continues:

Moreover, the inanimate is unconscious of being affected whereas the animate is conscious of it, though there is nothing to prevent the animate also being unconscious of it when the alteration does not concern the senses. Since then, the alteration of that which undergoes alteration is caused by sensible things, in every case of such alteration it is evident that the extremities of that which causes and that which undergoes alteration are together. For the air is continuous with the one, and also with the body. Again, colour is continuous with the light and the light with the eye—and similarly with hearing and smelling, for the primary agent of change in relation to what is changed is the air. Similarly in the case of taste, the flavour is together with the sense of taste. And it is just the same in the case of things which are inanimate and insensate. Thus, there can be nothing in between what is altered and what alters it. (244b15–245a11)

Everson, then, concludes on the basis of *Phys* 7.2 that perception involves alteration$_1$, which also applies to non-perceptual changes.

Both percipient and non-percipient patients will undergo a change which can be described in the same way. Both will be altered "by becoming hot or sweet or thick or dry or white." In both perceptual and non-perceptual alteration the patient is assimilated to the agent and takes on its property. In both cases, this will be a case of alteration$_1$.[37]

Everson seems to grant that what Aristotle says in the passage from *Phys* 7.2 may not be the only or final account that he will give on the relation between sense powers and their organs. "This chapter of the *Physics* is an interesting one, and unduly neglected in discussions of Aristotle's theory of perception, since it shows quite clearly that he was, at one point in his career, committed to the literalist account of perceptual change."[38] By the time he came to write the *DA*, Aristotle seems to have changed his mind on the point that is central to *Phys* 7.2, namely, the need for agent and patient to be in contact for the one to affect and the other to be affected. In *Phys*, he claims that the object is in contact with the medium and the medium with the eye, and the whole process is a straightforward one. On this account, one would expect that if the object were in direct contact with the eye, the alteration$_1$ that he describes there would occur even more easily. However, in the *DA*, Aristotle notes the fact that one cannot see in this case, that is, by placing an object directly on the eye, is evidence first that perception requires a medium in all cases, and second that, because of this, perception is not an alteration$_1$.[39] This divergence between the *DA* account and the *Phys* one will be examined again later.

Having argued that Aristotle's account of perception affirms that both kinds of alterations occur, Everson elaborates the relation between them. Although the two sorts of alteration are not each reducible to the other, and certainly not identifiable (as functionalism asserts), according to Everson's interpretation, the material change (alteration$_1$) nevertheless determines the psychological activity (alteration$_2$). He claims that this is necessarily implied in *Phys* 7.3, where Aristotle discusses why processes other than those caused by perceptible qualities are not alterations.[40]

And moreover, it would seem absurd to speak in such manner, to say, e.g., that a man or a house or anything else whatsoever that has come to be has undergone an alteration. But it is perhaps necessary for each of these to come to be when something else is altered, e.g., when the matter is thickened or thinned or heated or cooled, the things which come to be are not altered and their coming into being is not alteration. (246a4–9)[41]

When a man or a house comes to be, the man or house is not altered since it only has just come to exist; its coming to be, however, may have been necessitated by matter undergoing alteration$_1$. Similarly, bodily *hexeis*, such as health and fitness, are not alterations, nor is their acquisition and loss, but "it is perhaps necessary that they come to be and are destroyed when certain other things undergo alteration, just as in the case of substantial and geometrical forms" (246b14–15).[42]

The formula Aristotle uses for the genesis of substances, bodily *hexeis*, and virtues and vices is that when the relevant alteration (or alterations) occurs, then the higher-level change *must* occur. . . . If this is right, then Aristotle commits himself here to the determination of changes at the formal level by alterations at the material level.[43]

Thus, alterations in the matter determine and necessitate the coming to be (which is not an alteration) of things having a new form—substantial, geometrical or dispositional.

Having grounded his interpretation on the basis of these texts, Everson seeks to clarify his position by appealing to another notion popular in the contemporary philosophy of mind, that is, supervenience. To the extent that material changes determine formal changes,[44] this interpretation claims that alterations$_2$ supervene on alterations$_1$; the psychological process supervenes on the material change. As Everson explains, an event is said to supervene on another if a difference among events of the first sort cannot occur without a difference of events of the second sort. If the material determines the formal in Aristotle's theory, there can be no difference in the formal aspect of perception without a difference in the material aspect. Consequently, Everson argues that for Aristotle, the formal supervenes on the material.

On Everson's interpretation, Aristotle happily is in agreement with a contemporary theory fulfilling physicalist aspirations. For if the formal or mental supervenes on the material or physical, there is not even token identity of the mental with the physical, wherein some particular mental state is identified with a given physical state. As such, this interpretation avoids a major problem of another contemporary theory claiming for itself the authority of an Aristotelian precedent, that is, functionalism. Functionalism, it will be remembered, defines a mental state as a physical state playing the necessary causal role. Supervenience, in contrast, claims that the different levels of causality, that is, the mental and the physical, are irreducible to each other. Causal relations are within, rather than between, these levels, such that a given mental state may cause other mental states (e.g., anger may cause the desire for retaliation) parallel to the level at which physical states cause other physical states (e.g., boiling of the blood may cause the contraction of muscles). One can thus claim that the mental level is determined by the physical without (as yet) specifying how it is determined. There is, then, the promise of reduction without the need to explain the mechanism by which the mental is determined by the physical. Thus, physical events provide both the necessary and sufficient condition for the occurrence of mental events, without the latter being strictly reducible to the former.

TEXTUAL OBJECTIONS TO EVERSON AND SUPERVENIENCE

Believing that both kinds of alterations are involved in perception and that alterations$_2$ supervene on alterations$_1$ creates difficulties in interpreting Aristotle. First, Everson claims that the change in the organ is not strictly perception. Rather, the subject perceives by becoming aware of the alteration taking place in the sense organ.[45] It is a curious element of Everson's interpretation of Aristotle, then, that one is not aware of a sensible quality as it belongs to an external object, but only as that quality is in the organ.

On Aristotle's account, in contrast, the red of which one is aware when one perceives something is not some mental item, or property thereof, but the modification of something straightforwardly material. What one is aware of *is* the redness of the object which affects the eye, since that is the colour which the eye has taken on when affected by it and one is aware of the affection of the eye.[46]

One is directly aware of a bodily affection, that is, of the αἴσθημα, and by means of this awareness, one perceives the external object. Everson believes this view is confirmed by how Aristotle distinguishes between the activities of imagination and perception. Citing *On Dreams* (*Ins*), Everson says: "So at 460b2–3 we are told that 'even when the external sense-object has gone, the *aisthemata* [that is, the perceptual affections], which are objects of perception, remain."[47] This reading of the text is not insignificant, however, since Everson uses it to show that in both imagination and perception one is aware of bodily affections, and that the difference between them for Aristotle is their causal history. He reiterates the point a few pages later when he says: "We have already seen that in the *Ins*, Aristotle takes the *aisthemata* themselves to be *aistheta*, objects of perception (460b2–3)."[48] He then summarizes what he takes to be Aristotle's view of the perceptual process: "The external object acts on the sense organ so as to produce an *aisthema*, which is then transmitted to the central organ. The subject perceives the external object because he is aware of that *aisthema*." Everson elucidates in a note:

Wedin (1988), 37, comments that "Ordinarily *I* am not aware of the perceptual state, or *aisthema*, but only of the truck." This, however, confuses what it is to be an object of awareness with what it is to be an object of perception. Ordinarily I will perceive the truck but will do so in virtue of being aware of the *aisthema*. What is represented as being in front of me is the truck and that is indeed what I have beliefs about if I assent to the perception. This is quite consistent with the fact that it is the *aisthema* which is the object of awareness.[49]

Everson apparently believes that the representational features of affections are such that when one is aware of the affection, one perceives the object that gave rise to that affection.

That his view of Aristotle's theory of perception results in what is essentially an indirect realist theory of sense knowledge is at least an indication that Everson is misreading things.[50] This theory, as thus presented, opens up some epistemological space for perceivers to fail in attaining their objects should the affection not resemble whatever causes it. Indeed Everson believes that Aristotle holds to this theory precisely in order to account for such perceptual failures. But Aristotle also clearly believes that one directly perceives the proper objects of sensation, and the only evidence offered for the indirectness of perception, that is, *Ins* 2, 460b2–3, is far from conclusive in its support for Everson's interpretation. The Greek reads ἀπελθόντος τοῦ θύραθεν αἰσθητοῦ ἐμμένει τὰ αἰσθήματα αἰσθητὰ ὄντα, and J. I. Beare translates it as "even when the external object of perception has departed, the impressions it has made persist, and are themselves objects of perception." It seems clear that the affections to the organs, αἰσθήματα, become objects of perception *only when* the external object departs, for the examples from which Aristotle concludes this general principle are all cases where an affection of the eye only becomes visible after one's vision has shifted from the object that causes it, such as the sun or a flowing river (459b8–23). It seems totally gratuitous, then, for Everson to offer a reading of this line wherein αἰσθήματα are *normally* objects of perception. This passage from *Ins* is not the only passage of Aristotle's that is altered to fit the literalist/supervenience reading of perception.

For despite Everson's assertions to the contrary, *DA* 2.5 does indeed, on the most natural reading, rule out perception being or even involving alteration₁ Aristotle, describing the difference between the two kinds of alteration (i.e., between alteration properly so called and that sort of alteration that should have its own name), says that when someone learns and passes from potential knowledge to actual knowledge under the influence of someone who has actual knowledge, this process

either ought not to be described as "being acted upon," as has been said, or else there are two senses of alteration, one a change to a negative condition (alteration₁), and the other a change to a positive state, that is, a realization of its nature (alteration₂). In sentient creatures (τοῦ δ᾽ αἰσθητικοῦ) the first change (alteration₁) is caused by the male parent, and at birth the subject has sensation in the sense in which we spoke of the mere possession of knowledge. Actual perception corresponds to exercise of knowledge. (417b12–22)[51]

Here Aristotle is delineating the extent to which both kinds of alteration pertain to sensation. Alteration$_1$ applies to the process of changing from a potential$_1$ sensor to an actual$_1$/potential$_2$ sensor, and it is accomplished under the agency of the animal's sire. Alteration$_2$ applies to the processes of changing from a potential$_2$ sensor to an actual$_2$ sensor. There is no indication that an alteration$_1$ is involved in the case of a sense organ, and alteration$_2$ applies to the sense power. To believe that Aristotle, after this explication of how the two kinds of alteration function for perceivers, meant to leave the possibility open that alteration$_1$ is still operative in perception on a material level would seem to imply extreme carelessness in Aristotle's explanation.

Moreover, this passage seems clear in its indication that perception is *only* an alteration$_2$. When Aristotle says that "actual perception corresponds to the exercise of knowledge" (417b22), he has just equated the exercise of knowledge with alteration$_2$ (417b5). Since the point of the chapter is, as Everson admits, to contrast the two senses of alteration, Aristotle's assertion that actual perception is an alteration$_2$ clearly implies that it is not, nor is there any reason to think that it "involves," an alteration$_1$. That this is the correct way to read *DA* 2.5 is also confirmed in *DA* 3.7:

And clearly the sensible object makes the sense-faculty (αἰσθητικοῦ) actually operative from being only potential; it is not acted upon, nor does it undergo change of state (οὐ γὰρ πάσχει οὐδ᾽ ἀλλοιοῦται); and so, if it is motion, it is motion of a distinct kind; for motion, as we saw, is an activity of the imperfect, but activity in the absolute sense, that is, activity of the perfected, is different. (431a4–8)[52]

As will become clear, however, it would be a mistake to assume, with the spiritualists, that because perception is only an alteration$_2$, it is therefore in no sense a physical process that the organs of sense undergo. Indeed, Aristotle believes that there are some manifestly physical, as opposed to mental, processes that are not motions, that is, alterations$_1$, but are instead activities, that is, alterations$_2$.

Besides inconclusive general statements by Aristotle that animal bodies are composed ultimately of elements, the only evidence for the claim that Aristotle endorses explaining psychological events and processes by invoking both material and formal causes comes from *DA* 1.1.[53] In this chapter, among other things, Aristotle tries to parse out whether there are any affections that belong to the soul alone. After making some concessions to the difficulties posed by νοῦς, Aristotle concludes: "It seems that these affections of the soul are associated with the body— anger, gentleness, fear, pity, courage and joy; as well as loving and hating; for when they appear the body is also affected" (403a17–19).[54] More than being merely simultaneous with psychic affections, he apparently believes that bodily dispositions have a significant influence on the kind and extent of affections of the soul that a person suffers. He gives as examples both the fact that a small provocation to a person in the appropriate bodily condition can cause anger and the fact that a person can have fear by being in another bodily condition without any cause (403a19–24). He concludes that because the affections are so connected with the body, they are "forms in matter" (403a25–26).[55]

It is at this point that Everson claims that Aristotle spells out the program of specifying the material causes of psychological processes in distinction from their formal cause, for Aristotle goes on to explain what such definitions of affections of the soul should include in order to be in harmony with the fact that they are forms in matter (λόγοι ἔνυλοι). "And so their (affections') definitions should be likewise, just as anger is defined as some movement of a body, or of a part or power of a body, from a given cause, for the sake of a given end" (403a26–28).[56] As Aristotle elaborates, it is clear that the movement of a body, for example, surging of the blood and heat around the heart, specifies the matter of anger and that this sort of a definition of anger is appropriate to the (traditional) philosopher of nature. Form, for example, a craving for retaliation, on the other hand, is specified by the dialectician's definition (403a28–403b4). Aristotle, then, concludes that the complete definition will include both the form and the matter, just as the complete definition of a house specifies that it is a shelter against wind, rain and heat, finding realization in stones, bricks and timbers (403b4–9). With this distinction in hand, Everson feels justified in identifying the matter of perception as an alteration occurring in the sense organ, and the form as the activity that supervenes on this alteration. He holds to this distinction in the kinds of changes that animate substances undergo despite his assertion that "the *psuche* and the body are not separate individual substances which can be affected together. There is only one affectable substance and that is the living thing which is the composite of *psuche* and body."[57] Indeed, it is Everson's position that both are separately specifiable for "whenever there is a formal change, there will be a material change (or material changes) which determines it."[58] Everson believes that only by positing these two sorts of changes can one make sense of the material requirements for organs that Aristotle repeatedly insists upon.

The *kore* [pupil of the eye] needs to be transparent because colours are such as to bring about change in what is transparent. This change is a change which, in respect of the *kore*, is a material change. Because the transparent stuff in question is part of a suitable complex physiological system, the colour is able not only to produce this material change but also to bring about the activity of vision. That second change is a psychological and hence formal change.[59]

The unity of the matter/form composite for Aristotle, however, does not allow there to be a material cause of a process as opposed to its formal cause. Upon examining this first chapter of *DA*, Aristotle's endorsement of material and formal explanations are not so straightforward. In *DA* 1.1, Aristotle says that affections are shared (κοινὰ) by both the soul and what contains it (the body) (403a5). This seems to mean that each affection belongs to both the body and the soul and there is not a physical process for one and a mental act for the other. Furthermore, although Aristotle says that the true natural philosopher bases his definition on what both the dialectician says (form) and on what the (traditional) natural philosopher says (matter) (ἣ δε μᾶλλον ὁ ἐξ ἀμφοῖν—403b9), he does not produce two definitions of anger, or even one definition with two parts, but only one definition that is based on both the dialectician's and the traditional natural philosopher's. Aristotle's point does not seem to be that the natural philosopher merely combines the dialectician's and the physicist's definitions into his own, but that his definition takes account of facts relevant to the other two, while being itself one definition of one event.

Furthermore, there is independent evidence that Aristotle's theoretical framework does not allow an animal's matter to undergo a different process than its form, even though it is true that Aristotle gives descriptions of things in terms of their matter. Again in *GC*, Aristotle considers the difficulties raised by saying that material constituents "combine" to form another substance distinct from them. If the constituents persist after being combined, then nothing has really happened to them, that is, nothing new has resulted; if one or both of the constituents are destroyed, then what results cannot be attributed to them since they no longer exist (327a35–b7). It appears contradictory to say that the parts of substances are actually substances, on the one hand, and just plain false to say the parts of substances are not combined in a substance, on the other. Anything one calls a substance cannot have other actual substances as parts, for then two substances would be in the same place at the same time, and the same thing would be two things, in the same respect, that is, as an actual substance. Thus, a certain piece of matter, say a bone, would be actually and substantially both an animal and earth (a non-animal) at the same time; but it also seems wrong to say that bones are not made of earth.

Aristotle's solution is to propose a theory of the continued presence of the constituents by means of their powers. Instead of allowing the parts to exist in the combined substance with the full actuality of substances, Aristotle says that these other substances, that is, the elements, in a sense are and in a sense are not in the combined substance; they exist potentially in the substances into which they changed.

Since, however, some things *are-potentially* while others *are-actually*, the constituents combined in a compound can "be" in a sense and yet "not-be." The compound may *be-actually* other than the constituents from which it has resulted; nevertheless, each of them may *be-potentially* what it was before they were combined, and both of them may survive undestroyed. . . . The constituents, therefore, neither *persist actually*, as "body" and "white" persist: nor are they *destroyed* (either one of them or both), for their "power of action" is preserved. (*GC* 1.10, 327b23–26, 29–31)

Since "matter" is the principle of potency, the matter of the elements becomes the matter of the substance they compose, but the elements are present potentially in the newly composed substance. So, while there is only one substance that results from the composition of various elements, the new substance has the powers of the elements that came together in its composition. Aquinas elaborates Aristotle's theory, saying that the elements are not actually in the substance, but they are there virtually, that is, by their power (*virtus*).

Therefore we must say, in accordance with the Philosopher, that forms of the elements remain in the mixed body, not actually, but virtually. For the proper qualities of the elements remain, though modified; and in these qualities is the power of the elementary forms. This quality of the mixture is the proper disposition for the substantial form of the mixed body; for instance, the form of a stone, or of any sort of soul.[60]

Thus, while a substance may act in virtue of the material elements that compose it, it is the substance that acts and not the elements; nor do elements have their own distinct activities.[61] Thus, while an eye is affected in virtue of the water it contains, there is only one process that takes place, and what happens to the water is the same process as what happens to the power of vision that makes the water to be (part of) an eye.

With this theoretical apparatus in place, one can understand that when Aristotle says in *DA* 1.1 that the natural philosopher's definition of psychic affections includes both the form and the matter, he is not advocating that such affections have both a formal cause and a material cause, much less that one could be a process or event of one type (a motion) and the other an event of a contrary type (an activity). The definition of the affection will account for all the relevant facts, including facts that derive from the matter of the animal that is the subject of the affection. In the case of perceptions, the one event will be seen to be an activity, but one that is conditioned by material consideration. This does not create a problem of mixing motions and activities in one event, since, as will become clear, for Aristotle some manifestly material and physical events are activities.

PHILOSOPHICAL OBJECTIONS TO SUPERVENIENCE

There are even more compelling reasons for believing that Aristotle could not accept that perceptual activity supervenes on physical alteration. For, the potency that the subject of an alteration$_1$ has at the beginning of the alteration$_1$ is completely actualized by the end, and at the end it is no longer in a state of potency with respect to the same sort of alteration$_1$. What is altered$_1$ is in potency to what it will become, but in so altering$_1$, it thereby loses that potency to be altered$_1$—that is, once it is altered$_1$, it cannot then be altered$_1$ again with respect to the same quality. This is the definition of alteration$_1$. If, however, sense organs were to be altered$_1$ in perception, they would then lose their capacity to be altered again.[62] Such a view of the physical process occurring in sense organs creates insuperable problems when it is connected to perception as an activity.[63]

On the literalist model, the eye, for instance, is made literally red in one instant, and in just one part of its eye-jelly. That part, in that instant, then loses the potency to be affected by red until the affection that is there fades. However, one would expect that, in the next instant, even before the red affection fades, it could be affected by a blue object, turning the formerly red bit of eye-jelly blue. This should hold true because the eye-jelly, even though affected by the red object, is still matter for a living, functioning eye; it, thus, should still have the capacity for sight. If it were true that red-ly affected eye-jelly bits can become blue, then one has abandoned Aristotle's principle that the eye-jelly be transparent in order to be affected by colors (*De Sensu* 2, 438a12–14). Clearly, then, this alternative is unacceptable.

However, if one denies that the red eye-jelly bit can become blue, on the other hand, and instead claims that the redness of the bit of eye-jelly must fade first, one still encounters problems. Such an account seems contrary to Aristotle's (and Everson's) commitment that perceptual awareness is a continuous activity. For, while looking at the same red wall, one does not ever cease to perceive it. If seeing occurs when the eye-jelly takes on the color of the object seen, however, one would not see the red wall for as long as it took the last moment's affection in the eye-jelly to fade. Perhaps, one could claim that eye-jelly affections fade rather quickly. In this case, while it is true that until the previous affection fades there would be no perceiving, perception would occur intermittently, producing a sort of strobing effect that might go undetected. However, insofar as perception at least involves an activity, it is continuous, and our ability to engage in it is constant, even while already being engaged in it. Thus, the formal cause of perception could not be a single activity if it has to supervene on the strobing of alterations in the organs, since it is at least necessary that what supervenes be simultaneous with what it supervenes on. Supervenience, then, cannot accommodate both standard alterations and activities in an Aristotelian explanation of perception.

The potency that characterizes a sense power in being potentially like its object, then, is a condition of perception that exists throughout the perceptual process. Thus, even while perceiving, the sense organ does not lose its capacity to perceive, and so it does not cease being able to become like its object. Aristotle seems to have had this in mind when he introduces the distinction between alteration properly so called and activity by saying that the activity of perception is a preserving one (417b3). Furthermore, Aristotle is able to present a consistent account of perception because he believes that the effect of light and color at least, and presumably by extension the effects of the objects of the other senses, are also activities that the physical organ engages in.

RECEIVING FORM WITHOUT MATTER

Spiritualists such as Burnyeat who have interpreted Aristotle's theory of perception as not being a case of ordinary alteration appeal to *DA* 2.12. In this chapter, Aristotle gives a general summary of his views on sensation and entertains some problems associated with it. It is here that he claims that all perception is a reception of form without matter, and employs the analogy of a gold signet ring impressing a block of wax, both of which seem to provide problems for the literalist interpreters.

> We must understand as true generally of every sense that sense is that which is receptive of sensible forms without matter, just as the wax receives the impression of the signet-ring without the iron or the gold, and receives the impression of the gold or bronze, but not as gold or bronze; so in every case sense is affected by that which has color, or flavor, or sound, but by it, not *qua* having a particular identity, but *qua* being such, and in virtue of its form. (*DA* 2.12, 424a17–24)

Here, Aristotle says that the sense receives form without matter, as the wax receives the impression without the iron or gold, but does not do so as gold or bronze. A few lines later, he elaborates somewhat on the meaning of "form without matter" when he considers how the passivity of the senses differs from the way in which insensate things are affected by the same sorts of objects.

> It is also clear why plants do not feel, though they have one part of the soul, and are affected to some extent by objects touched, for they show both cold and heat; the reason is that they have no mean, i.e., no first principle such as to receive the form of sensible objects, but are affected with the matter. (424a33–b3)

Plants apparently do not receive form without matter; instead they are affected with the matter since they have no "mean" or "principle" for the reception of form. To receive form without matter, then, requires being of the right physical constitution, described here as a "mean," which is the principle for such a reception. Although plants are affected by the objects of touch, that is, heat and cold, they are affected with matter, and this explains why they do not sense. Finally, Aristotle distinguishes the effect that sensible qualities have on inanimate things from their effects on perceivers. He considers whether a sensible quality, such as smell, affects anything besides a perceiver of smells, and answers that "it is impossible for anything which cannot smell to be affected by smell; and the same argument applies to the other senses" (424b7–8). However, he seems to change his mind, for he says that some things are affected by sensible qualities (424b12–17). He then asks, "What, then, is smelling apart from being affected in some way? Probably the act of smelling is also an act of perception, whereas the air, being only temporarily affected, merely becomes perceptible" (424b17–20). Both the air becoming smelly and an animal smelling it are cases of things being affected by smells, but when the animal is affected, it perceives; when the air is affected, there is no perception.

The proper interpretation of the idea of the reception of form without matter has been a major point of contention between literalists and spiritualists. Sorabji claims that the phrase refers exclusively to the organ becoming literally like its object, but this was shown to be false since Aristotle argues that the intellect also receives form without matter. The literal interpretation may yet be correct—that, in the case of sense, the reception of form without matter does in fact mean that the organ becomes literally assimilated to its object. Thus, literalists claim that the point of the analogy with the wax block and signet-ring in *DA* 2.12 is that the gold, that is, the matter of what makes the impression, is what is left behind. All that is received is the impression, but this impression is a literal and physical impression in the wax. Likewise, the sense organ receives the sensible form of its object, that is, it comes to have literally in itself that sensible form.

But there is good reason to interpret the reception of form without matter physiologically. It means that, for instance, the organ of sight . . . takes on the colour of the object seen, without taking on any material particles from the object, such as Empedocles and Democritus had postulated.[64]

Sorabji, then, points to the fact that at the end of *DA* 2.12 (424b17–20), when Aristotle says that smelling is also a perceiving, he is saying that perceiving is also a material alteration that the organ, like the air, undergoes.[65] Because inanimate things undergo the same alterations that perceivers do, the process undergone by perceivers, the receiving form without matter, is a physical alteration, which means that the organ of the perceiver becomes literally the same as its object. Thus, when plants are said to become hot or cold by being affected with the matter, they do so by receiving small particles or vapors of the agent that is making them hot; "plants become warm by letting warm air or other warm matter into their systems, instead of leaving the matter behind."[66]

Aquinas, insofar as he is said to side with the spiritualists, predictably has a different account of what Aristotle means by the reception of form without matter. In his *Commentary on the* De Anima, he entertains the objection that receiving form without matter does not seem to be unique to sensation since in non-perceptual cases of a thing being affected, the patient also receives the form of the agent without its matter.[67] Aquinas explains that although in an ordinary case of being passively affected a thing does receive the form without the agent's matter, the patient still receives form with matter, that is, within its own matter, since the recipient's matter "becomes, in a way, the same as the material agent, inasmuch as it acquires a material disposition like that which was in the agent."[68] He argues, then, that the reception of form without matter is in contrast to the patient taking on the quality in the same sense, that is, in a material sense, as the agent.

Sometimes, however, the recipient receives the form into a mode of existence other than that which the form has in the agent; when, that is, the recipient's material disposition to receive form does not resemble the material disposition in the agent. In these cases the form is taken into the recipient "without matter," the recipient being assimilated to the agent in respect of form and not in respect of matter. And it is thus that a sense receives form without matter, the form having, in the sense, a different mode of being from that which it has in the object sensed. In the latter it has a material mode of being, but in the sense, a cognitional and spiritual mode.[69]

When the form is in the patient in a way other than as that form is in the agent's material disposition, then the patient is assimilated in a way that is not standardly material. The fact that this second way differs from the first, that is, material, mode is what warrants calling it "without matter." In this second mode, however, it is still the recipient's material disposition that does not resemble the agent's; thus, the fact that Aquinas calls the manner in which form is in the sense a "spiritual" mode should not distract from the fact that even he believes that this takes place in the organ: "the organ of sense is that in which a power of this sort resides, namely a capacity to receive forms without matter."[70] In contrast to Burnyeat's spiritualist interpretation, the reception of form without matter is a physical process for Aquinas to the extent that it takes place in the physical organ. He believes, then, that the second mode of receptivity, that is, coming to have the quality but not according to the agent's disposition, is what Aristotle means to convey by the wax block example.

The force of the wax block example, for Aquinas, is that the shape of the signet-ring comes to be in the wax, but not in the same respect as it is in the signet-ring. Finding significant the fact that Aristotle says that the seal is received both without the gold and not as gold, Aquinas comments, "hence wax, he says, takes a sign, i.e., a shape or image, of what is gold or bronze, but not precisely as gold or bronze. For the wax takes a likeness of the gold seal in respect of the image, but not according to the disposition of gold."[71] It seems that, for Aquinas, the fact that the image received is a negative or reverse of the seal (and so the wax has the image but not as the gold has it) is analogous to what is distinctive of sensation—that is, the fact that the image is in the wax in a different way than it is in the ring illustrates the fact that the sensible form is in the organ in a way different than it is in the object. For, the wax does not have the image to the extent that it can cause another impression, and so it is not a seal-like image; it lacks "the seal's intrinsic disposition to be a gold seal." Analogously, sense organs do not take on the forms of their sensible objects to the extent that they can again be perceived; the sense

is not affected by a colored stone precisely as stone, or sweet honey precisely as honey, because in the sense there is no such disposition to the form as there is in these substances; but it is affected by them precisely as colored, or tasty, or as having this or that "informing principle" or form.[72]

Since literalists offer no other explanation of Aristotle's words "without the gold and not as gold," it seems that Aquinas's reading accounts for more of the text, and reflects Aristotle's intention. Plants, then, "are affected and undergo changes only materially."[73]

Everson defends Sorabji and the literalist interpretation by pointing to what Aristotle says about the physical constitution of plants. According to Everson, plants in Aristotle's theory are not made hot or cold by taking on the forms of these qualities, but by admitting hot or cold matter. This is what Aristotle means when he says that plants are affected with the matter. Everson, to support this radical contention, cites *DA* 3.13, where Aristotle says that "touch is a kind of mean between all tangible qualities, and its organ is receptive not only of all the different qualities of earth, but also of hot and cold, and all other tangible qualities" (435a22–24). Plants, however, because they are made of earth, do not have a mean for the tangible qualities that belong to the elements other than earth, and this fact explains their insensitivity. As Aristotle says: "And for this reason plants have no sensation, because they are composed of earth" (435b1–3). Everson argues that Aristotle's reasoning rests on the claim that earth can itself have no qualities other than the cold and dry; these are essential to being earth: "an element cannot lose its distinctive qualities without ceasing to be that element."[74] He cites *GC* 2.3 to support this contention. If earth, or something made of earth, appears warm or moist, it is because it has taken into itself some other matter with these qualities.

> The force of the claim that plants are affected with the matter is not, then, that plants are affected by both the form and the matter of whatever heats them up: they are not affected by the form at all since their own matter is incapable of taking on the property of, say, heat. . . . [S]trictly, the plant itself is not affected at all.[75]

Thus, according to Everson, plants do not undergo alteration at all and do not take on the form of the agent in their own matter. Instead, they take on some of the matter of the agent that has the sensible form in question.

Unfortunately, this view of how plants take on various sensible qualities is at variance with other texts of Aristotle, texts quite central to Everson's overall argument. First, *Phys* 7.2, which Everson cites to show that the alterations involved in perception are suffered also by insensate things, clearly shows that plants do undergo alteration even in respect to tangible qualities.

> Thus we say that a thing is altered by becoming hot or sweet or thick or dry or white; and we make these assertions alike of what is inanimate and what is

animate. And further, where animate things are in question, we make them both of the parts that have no power of perception and the senses themselves. (244b6–10)

Thus, in this passage, which Everson makes use of in his general argument, plants, that is, animate things without perception, are altered and become, among other things, hot and dry. It appears, then, that the fact that plants are made of earth does not in fact prevent their being literally heated and cooled. Since Aristotle says here that plants become hot by being altered, he cannot think that this happens by their taking on the matter of what heats or cools them.

Moreover, Aristotle explicitly rejects those theories that explain the apparent changes in quality of things by postulating a process and mechanism by which matter enters into the things that are so affected. In *GC* 1.8, Aristotle considers the view of those philosophers who believe that an agent "enters through certain pores, and so the patient suffers action" (324b26). While these thinkers postulated this theory to account for sense perception, Aristotle presents the theory as being quite general and evaluates it in general terms that have nothing to do with the problems peculiar to sense perception. Furthermore, he specifically mentions Empedocles (324b33) and Leucippus and Democritus (325a1) as proponents of this theory. He is extremely critical of these views, however, in spite of the suggestion by Sorabji that Aristotle would have advocated such a theory.

If an agent produces no effect by touching the patient, neither will it produce any effect by passing through its pores. On the other hand, if it acts by contact, then—even without pores—some things will "suffer action" and others will "act," provided they are by nature adapted for reciprocal action and passion. (326b22–24)

So even though his predecessors held to the view that things change their sensible characteristics by taking on the matter of an agent of this change, Aristotle explicitly rejects it in *GC* 1.8. While it is true that Aristotle believed that the explanations of perception offered by Empedocles and Democritus, which considered the use of pores to be inadequate, his criticism against pore theories in *GC* opposes such theories as an explanation of all action and passion, not just of perception. It is extremely unlikely he would have changed his position in the *DA* when it comes to explaining the heating and cooling of plants.

Another part of *GC* 2.3 shows that Aristotle does not believe that the material constitution of plants prevents them from being altered in respect to tangible qualities. Ironically, after appealing to this chapter to show that anything composed purely of earth cannot itself be made hot or cold since earth is essentially cold and dry, Everson uses it as his basis for concluding that the fact that plants are composed of earth must mean that they are heated and cooled by receiving hot or cold matter. He is right, of course, that the elements do have these qualities essentially. "For Fire is hot and dry, whereas Air is hot and moist (Air being a sort of aqueous vapour); and Water is cold and moist, while Earth is cold and dry" (330b4–5). A few lines later, however, Aristotle warns that, although he takes the four traditional elements into his system, one should not believe that these "simple bodies" are to be found in nature in a pure form. "In fact, however, fire and air, and each of the bodies we have mentioned, are not simple, but blended. The 'simple' bodies are indeed similar in nature to them, but not identical with them" (330b20). Thus, the simple body of earth, that is, the element, is not the earth of our common experience, but similar to it. The earth of common experience and *a fortiori* things of experience made of earth are in fact not simple, but blended. There is, then, no theoretical obstacle to ordinary earth undergoing alteration and receiving the form of heat, say, from an agent, though this would be received into the earth's matter. So while Aristotle does say that plants are made of earth, it is safe to assume that he means that they, like other things of ordinary experience that are called earth, are blended with other elements. Thus, the claim that they do not feel because they are made of earth and are affected with matter means that they are made too much of earth to be a mean, and so cannot be affected in the non-material way that is characteristic of sense organs.

Therefore, just on the basis of *DA* 2.12, when the organ receives form without matter, it receives the same form as its object, but not as that form is in the object. Aristotle is explicit that sense is like the wax that receives an impression both without gold and not as gold. The literalists offer no interpretation for this qualification. In fact, the qualification seems to invalidate their interpretation since on their interpretation both the wax, on the one hand, has the shape just as the gold has it, and the sense organ, on the other hand, has the sensible quality just as the object has it, that is, literally. Aquinas, at least, explains Aristotle's qualification as indicating that the organ does not receive the form in a material way, that is, as an alteration. Furthermore, there is no warrant for believing that Aristotle accepted that a plant's being affected with matter means taking on some material vapor from the apparent agent. There are at least three places where he either implicitly or explicitly rejects this. The alternate interpretation, that of Aquinas, accommodates the view that a sense organ does not receive the matter of the object (which the literalists claim is Aristotle's sole point), since in no kind of alteration does the agent receive the matter of the agent, much less does a sense organ receive the matter of its object.[76]

Opposition to the literalist interpretation of the theory of the reception of form without matter should not be seen as capitulation with the spiritualists, however. Unlike Burnyeat, Aquinas holds that the reception of form without matter nevertheless takes place *in material organs.* Aristotle also explicitly applies the theory to sense organs, and so the theory must be meant to identify a physical process, but one that is not an alteration in the normal sense. In *DA* 3.2 (425b22–24), Aristotle claims that it is the *sense organ* of sight that is receptive of form without matter. Given that the theory of reception of form without matter is not alteration, this implies that what goes on in the organ is the same as what goes on in the power. "Sensation would seem to be a single alteration of the ensouled body which is a living functioning sense organ."[77] Thus, neither spiritualists nor literalists seem to capture Aristotle's intention that perception is a physical process that is nevertheless not an ordinary, that is, standard material, alteration. Aristotle believes that perception is an activity that is realized in sense organs.

THE MEDIUM OF SENSATION

Perhaps the biggest obstacle to accepting the literalist interpretation is that it seems so counter-intuitive. If color is in the eye in exactly the same sense as it is in the colored object, it seems impossible to reconcile this position with the claim that the transparent medium takes on color in the same sense as the eye does (for the eye does so in virtue of the transparency of the water it contains). For it is hard to see how color is "literally" in either the eye or the medium since it is clearly not in the medium in the same sense that it is in the colored object. Everson seems sensitive to this objection, for while he says that the water in the eye goes red when one sees a red object, thus emphasizing the literalist contention, he later says that the water in the eye becomes red in the same sense as a bowl of water.[78] If the example of a bowl of water becoming colored by a colored object is supposed to be illustrative of the sort of physical process that organs undergo, then this physical process hardly seems to be as straightforward as the term "literal" suggests. A bowl of water does not cease to be transparent and does not become literally as red as the object that is seen through it. What can be said for the bowl of water also can be said for the transparent medium, and so likewise for the eye. Since Aristotle believes that a medium is required for each of the senses, and by extension of what seems obvious in the case of color and sight, it seems that none of the sense organs literally take on the qualities of their organs.

Indeed, the fact that different objects can be seen through the same medium seems to indicate that the medium cannot become literally colored in the same sense as the object seen through it. If the medium has the color of the object seen through it, and Aristotle says it does, then the same medium would have contrary colors in it insofar as two perceivers see two objects with contrary colors through the same medium. For instance, suppose two people are facing two walls, a red one and a blue one, with each wall at a right angle to the other, so that the two people and the two walls form a square. In this situation, the line of sight of the person facing the red wall intersects the line of sight of the person facing the blue wall. If the coloring of the eye is like the coloring of the medium, and both are literal colorings, then it would be physically impossible for both people to see their respective walls, since the same medium, that is, the point at which the lines of sight intersect, would be both red and blue. Sorabji has cited this problem as one occasion for the commentary tradition's developing the spiritualist understanding out of what he believes is Aristotle's literalist theory. However, this seems to be a real problem for the literalist interpretation, for it seems that it is not merely that the medium does not in fact become literally colored, but that it could not in principle become colored in the ordinary way.

There is another peculiarity about perception, that is, the case of several perceivers perceiving the same object, that indicates that even the process occurring in the sense organ could not be an ordinary alteration. Sorabji also claims that this problem contributed to the ancient commentators' development of the spiritualist thesis, but it was in fact faced by Aristotle in *De Sensu*.

> But some find a further difficulty in this; for they say that it is impossible for one person to hear or see or smell the same thing as another; for they argue that it is impossible for several separate persons to hear or smell the same thing; for in that case a single thing would be separate from itself. The original cause of the movement, *e.g.*, the bell, or the incense, or the fire, which all perceive, is the same and numerically one, but the subjective perceptions (αἰσθάνονται) though specifically the same, are numerically different, for many see, smell, or hear at the same time. These are not bodies, but are an affection or movement of some kind (for otherwise the effect would not be what it is), though they imply body. (*De Sensu* 6, 446b17–27)[79]

In this passage, Aristotle is clear at least that the affections of perceivers are not bodies, but are "affections or movements" that imply body. This seems to indicate that they are straightforwardly alterations that the perceivers suffer. However, if that were the case, Aristotle would be granting the objection, and the various perceivers would have numerically different affections. It seems, however, that he is denying the objection, and when he says they are movements "of some kind," he is qualifying the sense in which they are alterations, indicating that if they are, they are not a straightforward kind. However, the fact that the perception is of one and the same object shows that the affection of the perceivers (in their organs) is not an ordinary alteration, for in that case, *ex hypothesi*, it would not be of one object, but of several. Thus, in order for the perceivers to actually perceive one object, they have to be affected in a way that is not an ordinary affection, and in the case under consideration, it is granted that they do perceive the one object. Therefore, although it is an affection of some kind, the process that a perceiver undergoes is not an ordinary alteration.

A further indication that perception, as it involves the sense organs, is not an ordinary alteration is found in several passages in *DA* where Aristotle gives an explanation of why all of the senses need a medium. His clearest example of a sense that requires a medium is the sense of sight, and Aristotle argues that the reason that a medium is required for the eye to see is the fact that color by itself, in coming into contact with the eye, does not produce vision. "The evidence for this is clear; for if one puts that which has color against the eye itself, it will not be visible.

Color moves the transparent medium, *e.g.*, the air, and this, being continuous, acts on the sense organ" (419a12–15). Likewise, in the case of the other senses, direct contact of the sense object with the organ does not produce perception (419a25–33). This reasoning holds even for the sense of touch, where physical contact indeed appears necessary; his most general assertion of this rationale is, in fact, found in his discussion of the sense of touch: "We perceive all things through a medium; but in this case (touch) it is not obvious" (423b7–8).

> In general, it seems that flesh and the tongue are related to the sense organ of touch as air and water are related to vision, hearing and smell. In neither case would sensation result from touching the sense organ; for instance, if one were to put a white body on the eye. From this it is clear that the organ of the tangible is within. Thus would occur what is also true in the other cases; for when objects are placed on the other sense organs no sensation occurs, but when they are placed on the flesh it does; hence the medium of the tangible is flesh. (423b18–27)

Aristotle is clear in *DA* (424b13–14), *GC* and *Phys* 7.2, however, that the sensible qualities produce alteration by contact. Therefore, color in the medium, although it is called a movement or motion, is not an alteration, but an activity.

The relationship between light and the perception of color that occurs by means of it indicates that the effect of color on both the medium of sight and the organ is not an alteration, but an activity. Color is not seen without light, "for, as we saw, it is the essence of colour to produce movement in the actually transparent; and the actuality of the transparent is light" (419a9–12). Thus, the physical nature that is common to the "everlasting upper firmament," air and water or whatever can be transparent, is made actually transparent by the activity of light (418b7–9). This physical nature when so actualized and made to be actually transparent receives the further actuality, that is, a "movement," from color. Although he sometimes calls the actuality of light a "movement," Aristotle clearly does not consider light itself, nor the color in the medium actualized by light, to be a literal movement, that is, an alteration. Rather, the actuality of light and of color occurs all at once and so could not be an alteration that travels through the transparent medium since the latter processes affect their subjects by stages.

Empedocles, and anyone else who has argued on similar lines is wrong in saying that light travels, spreading at a certain time between the earth and its envelope, without our noticing it; this is contrary both to the clear evidence of reason, and to the appearances; it would be possible for it to escape our observation in a small intervening space, but that it does so all the way between east and west is too large a claim. (418b21–27).

This line of reasoning is repeated in *De Sensu*, where Aristotle is explicit in his denial that light is a motion. There, he seems willing to grant that the media for the senses other than sight may involve motions that traverse the intervening space in a period of time. However, he explicitly denies that the medium of sight is made transparent in stages and that the colors of objects reach a midpoint between the object and the perceiver before reaching the perceiver. "With light there is a different account; for light is due to the existence of something, but is not a movement" (446b27–28). Here, Aristotle believes that for other senses the medium is not affected simultaneously, "except in the case of light, for the reason given, and of vision too for the same reason; for light causes vision" (447a11). Both light and vision are not the sorts of processes that progress through space for the same reason, namely, neither is a motion. Consequently, if color under the suitable conditions, that is, in a medium that is made actually transparent by light, brings about actual vision, it is also not a motion, but is in the medium in the same sense as light is. Therefore, since color is in the eye in the same sense as it is in the medium (for this is the reason that the eye must be made of a transparent substance), the coloration of the eye, the organ, is an activity (alteration$_2$), not a normal alteration (alteration$_1$).

Because one sees not only colors, but also sources of illumination such as the sun and fire, these luminous objects of sight give further evidence that vision does not come about from the eye undergoing an alteration. For, light is an activity, and as such, it not only actualizes the transparent, but is also visible. "Now fire is visible in both darkness and light, and this is necessarily so; for it is because of the fire that the transparent becomes transparent" (419a23–25). If the activity of fire, for example, allows other things to be seen, Aristotle reasons that when it itself is seen, this will likewise be due to its nature as an activity. Aristotle clearly denies that the transparent medium, and so *a fortiori*, the transparent in the eye, undergoes an alteration as a result of light; light is the actuality of the actually transparent. Thus, when light itself is an object of vision, it will not be seen through the organ undergoing an alteration since nothing in the nature of light is either the source or subject of an alteration. Rather, the vision of fire, say, occurs when the eye of the perceiving animal engages in or receives the activity of the light of the fire.

Aristotle's insistence on the need for a medium for sensation in *DA*, then, implies that he has changed his position on the mechanics of perception since *Phys* 7. The fact that in *DA* he insists on a medium for all senses, and rejects simple contact, is enough to warrant rejecting *Phys* 7 as his ultimate position on the sort of alteration that he believes sensation to be. Since *Phys* 7.3 was Everson's primary evidence for Aristotle's adherence to supervenience (since in this chapter Aristotle says both that there are two kinds of alterations and that the physical determines the mental), we can reject Everson's claim that Aristotle endorsed supervenience.

CONCLUSION

From the foregoing, it should be clear that for Aristotle perception is not an ordinary physical process. Given what he says about the material constraints and operational failures to which the senses are subject, one cannot deny that perception occurs because sense organs are affected. Thus, perception is indisputably a physical process. However, it seems that this physical process in the organ is not an ordinary alteration. On the most natural reading of *DA* 2.5, Aristotle denies that perception either is or involves this ordinary sense of alteration, and any evidence offered to support a contrary conclusion is either inconclusive or makes Aristotle inconsistent. Moreover, the literalist interpretation, which asserts that perceptual awareness is a formal aspect and an activity that supervenes on material alterations that sense organs undergo, becomes incoherent when joined to core Aristotelian doctrines. Aristotle's requirement that the matter of the eye, for instance, be transparent in order to be affected by color cannot be reconciled with the claim that this matter becomes literally colored when seeing occurs. Likewise, claims that activities supervene on organs suffering ordinary alterations are equally irreconcilable with the nature of activities, that is, that activities are continuous and the ability to engage in them undiminished by already being so engaged. In addition to these interpretive and philosophical failures, the literal interpretation of *DA* 2.12 championed by Everson and Sorabji is contradicted by other central texts of Aristotle. In order to account for more of the text, it seems best to interpret Aristotle's assertion that senses receive form without matter to mean that perception is a non-ordinary sort of physical process. Thus, the sense organs are the subject of their own physical activities, which Aristotle understands to be opposed to ordinary physical alterations. That this activity constitutes perception is confirmed by Aristotle's insistence that all the senses require a medium to unite them with their respective proper objects, as well as by his analysis of the activity involved in the fact that seeing is brought about by light. For all these reasons, it follows that Aristotle thought that perception is a special kind of physical process in order to account for what he saw as certain peculiarities about perceptual activity. These peculiarities, however, entail certain limitations on the activity of perception, limitations not shared by νοῦς, and ones that provide him with the theoretical basis for denying that the activity of νοῦς is realized in any part of the body.

NOTES

1. M. F. Burnyeat, "Is an Aristotelian Philosophy of Mind Still Credible? A Draft," in *Essays on Aristotle's* De Anima, ed. Martha C. Nussbaum and Amélie Oksenberg Rorty (Oxford: Clarendon Press, 1992), p. 19.

2. Ibid.

3. Ibid., p. 22.

4. Ibid., p. 21. Although he gives no specific reference to Aquinas, it seems that Burnyeat has the following text, or one like it, in mind: "Immutation is of two kinds, one natural, the other spiritual. Natural immutation takes place when the form of that which causes the immutation is received, according to its *natural* being, into the thing immuted, as heat is received into the thing heated. But spiritual immutation takes place when the form of what causes the immutation is received, according to a *spiritual* mode of being, into the thing immuted, as the form of color is received into the pupil which does not thereby become colored." Thomas Aquinas, *Summa Theologica*, I, q. 78, a. 3, in *Basic Writings of St. Thomas Aquinas*, ed. Anton Pegis (New York: Random House, 1945), p. 739.

5. Burnyeat, "Is an Aristotelian," p. 24.

6. Stephen Everson, *Aristotle on Perception* (Oxford: Clarendon Press, 1997), p. 10.

7. Ibid.

8. Ibid., pp. 80–81.

9. Ibid., p. 84.

10. Ibid., p. 81.

11. τὸ δὸ αἰσθητήριον αὐτῶν τὸ ἁπτικόν, καὶ ἐν ᾧ ἡ καλουμένη ἁφὴ ὑπάρχει αἴσθησις πρώτῳ, τὸ δυνάμει τοιοῦτόν ἐστι μόριον. τὸ γὰρ αἰσθάθεσθαι πάσχειν τι ἐστίν. ὥστε τὸ ποιοῦν, οἷον αὐτὸ ἐνεργείᾳ, τοιοῦτον ἐκεῖνο ποιεῖ, δυνάμει ὄν. διὸ τοῦ ὁμοίως θερμοῦ καὶ ψυχροῦ, ἢ σκληροῦ καὶ μαλακοῦ, οὐκ αἰσθανόμεθα, ἀλλὰ τῶν ὑπερβολῶν, ὡς τῆς αἰσθήσεως οἷον μεσότητός τινος οὔσης τῆς ἐν τοῖς αἰσθετοῖς ἐναντιώσεως. καὶ διὰ τοῦτο κρίνει τὰ αἰσθητά. τὸ γὰρ μέσον κριτικόν. γίνεται γὰρ πρὸς ἑκάτερον αὐτῶν θάτερον τῶν ἄκρων.

12. Everson, *Aristotle on Perception*, p. 82.

13. Ibid., pp 82–84.

14. Ibid., p. 84.

15. Ibid., pp. 84–85.

16. Jonathan Lear, *Aristotle and the Desire to Understand* (Cambridge: Cambridge University Press, 1988) pp. 114–115.

17. John E. Sisko, "Material Alteration and Cognitive Activity in Aristotle's *De Anima*," *Phronesis* 41, no. 2 (1996): 145–147.

18. Sisko, "Material Alteration," p. 145.

19. Ibid., p. 146.

20. Aristotle, *De Generatione Animalium*, vol. 1, trans. Arthur Platt, 780a3–5.

21. Sisko, "Material Alteration," pp. 146–147.

22. Cf. 417b12–22; 431a4–8; 477b11.

23. ἡ δ᾽, αἴσθησις ἐν τῷ κινεῖσθαί τε καὶ πάσχειν συμβαίνει, καθάπερ εἴρηται· δοκεῖ γὰρ ἀλλοίωσίς τις εἶναι.

24. οὐκ ἔστι δ᾽ ἀπλοῦν οὐδὲ τὸ πάσχειν, ἀλλὰ τὸ μὲν φθορά τις ὑπὸ τοῦ ἐναντίου, τὸ δὲ σωτηρία μᾶλλον τοῦ δυνάμει ὄντος ὑπὸ τοῦ ἐντελεχείᾳ ὄντος, καὶ ὁμοίου οὕτως ὡς δύναμις ἔχει πρὸς ἐντελέχειαν· θεωροῦν γὰρ γίγνεται τὸ ἔχον τὴν ἐπιστήμην, ὅπερ ἢ οὐκ ἔστιν ἀλλοιοῦσθαι (εἰς αὐτὸ γὰρ ἡ ἐπίδοσις καὶ εἰς ἐντελέχειαν) ἢ ἕτερον γένος ἀλλοιώσεως.

25. Everson, *Aristotle on Perception*, p. 92.

26. Ibid., pp. 95, 225.

27. καὶ τὸ κατ᾽ ἐνέργειαν δὲ ὁμοίως λέγεται τῷ θεωρεῖν.

28. Everson, "Aristotle on Perception," pp. 93–94.

29. Ibid., p. 90.

30. Ibid., pp. 93–94.

31. Ibid., p. 94.

32. It is unclear why Everson believes that the spiritualist position should maintain that the perceiver starts out being perceptible, since, according to Aristotle's principle it is supposed to start out *unlike* its object—that is, for the spiritualist, the object starts out capable of causing perception and comes to actually cause it.

33. Perhaps Everson does not believe there is any way to say that x has sensible quality S, other than to say something does or can perceive that x is S.

34. Lear, *Aristotle and the Desire*, p. 114.

35. Everson, *Aristotle on Perception*, pp. 94–95.

36. Ibid., p. 136.

37. Ibid., p. 137.

38. Ibid., p. 134.

39. Cf. 419a12–15; 419a25–33; 423b7–8; 423b18–27.

40. Sisko, "Material Alteration," pp. 142–143, also believes that *Phys* VII. 3 shows that a denial of material alteration is false.

41. ἔτι δὲ καὶ εἰπεῖν οὕτως ἄτοπον ἂν δόξειεν, ἠλλοιῶσθαι τὸν ἄνθρωπον ἢ τὴν οἰκίαν ἢ ἄλλο ὁτιοῦν τῶν γεγενημένων· ἀλλὰ γίγνεσθαι μὲν ἴσως ἕκαστον ἀναγκαῖον ἀλλοιουμένου τινός, οἷον τῆς ὕλης πυκνουμένης ἢ μανουμένης ἢ θερμαινομένης ἢ ψυχομενης, οὐ μέντοι τὰ γιγνόμενά γε ἀλλοιοῦται, οὐδ᾽ ἡ γένεσις αὐτῶν ἀλλοίωσίς ἐστιν.

42. ἀλλὰ γίγνεσθαι μὲν ἴσως αὐτὰς καὶ φθείρεσθαι ἀλλοιουμένων τινῶν ἀνάγκη, καθάπερ καὶ τὸ εἶδος καὶ τὴν μορφήν.

43. Everson, *Aristotle on Perception*, p. 271.

44. Ibid., p. 261.

45. Ibid., p. 137.

46. Ibid., p. 138.

47. Ibid., p. 175. Brackets are Everson's.

48. Ibid., p. 177.

49. Ibid., p. 87.

50. See Christopher Decaen, "The Viability of Aristotelian-Thomistic Color Realism," *The Thomist* 65 (2001): 179–222.

51. ἤτοι οὐδὲ πάσχειν φατέον, ὥσπερ εἴρηται, ἢ δύο τρόπυς εἶναι ἀλλοιώσεως, τήν τε ἐπὶ τὰς στερητικὰς διαθέσεις μεταβολὴν καὶ τὴν ἐπὶ τὰς ἕξεις καὶ τὴν φύσιν. τοῦ δ᾽ αἰσθητικοῦ ἡ μὲν πρώτη μεταβολὴ γίνεται ὑπὸ τοῦ γεννῶντος, ὅταν δὲ γεννηθῇ, ἔχει ἤδη ὥσπερ ἐπιστήμην καὶ τὸ αἰσθάνεσθαι. τὸ κατ᾽ ἐνέργειαν δὲ ὁμοίως λέγεται τῷ θεωρεῖν.

52. φαίνεται δὲ τὸ μὲν αἰσθητὸν ἐκ δυνάμει ὄντον τοῦ αἰσθητικοῦ ἐνεργείᾳ ποιοῦν· οὐ γὰρ πάσχει οὐδ᾽ ἀλλοιοῦται. διὸ ἄλλο εἶδος τοῦτο κινήσεως· ἡ γὰρ κίνησις τοῦ ἀτελοῦς ἐνέργεια, ἡ δ᾽ ἁπλῶς ἐνέργεια ἑτέρα, ἡ τετελεσμένου.

53. Everson, *Aristotle on Perception*, pp. 231–249.

54. ἔοικε δὲ καὶ τὰ τῆς ψυχῆς παθήματα εἶναι μετὰ σώματος, θυμός, πραότης, φόβος, ἔλεος, θάρσος, ἔτι χαρὰ καὶ τὸ φιλεῖν τε καὶ μισεῖν· ἅμα γὰρ τούτοις πάσχει τι τὸ σῶμα. This citation follows Jannone's text.

55. εἰ δ' οὕτως ἔχει, δῆλον ὅτι τὰ πάθη λόγοι ἔνυλοι εἰσιν.

56. ὥστε οἱ ὅροι τοιοῦτοι οἷον τὸ ὀργίζεσθαι κίνησίς τις τοῦ τοιουδὶ σώματος ἢ μέρους ἢ δυνάμεως ὑπὸ τοῦδε ἕνεκα τοῦδε.

57. Everson, *Aristotle on Perception*, p. 234.

58. Ibid., p. 282.

59. Ibid., p. 283.

60. Aquinas, *Summa Theologica*, I, q. 76, a. 4, ad 4, in *Basic Writings of Thomas Aquinas*, Anton C. Pegis (New York: Random House, 1945), p. 707.

61. See Christopher Decaen, "Elemental Virtual Presence in St. Thomas," *The Thomist* 64 (2000): 271–300.

62. Cf. James T. H. Martin, "Sense and Intentionality: Aristotle and Aquinas," in *Aquinas on Mind and Intellect: New Essays*, ed. Jeremiah Hackett (Oakdale, NY: Dowling College Press, 1996), p. 177.

63. Indeed, this seems to be Aristotle's point in *Meta* 10.6: an activity continues even after it is completely actualized, whereas a motion ceases upon the completion of its actualization. Cf. J. L. Ackrill, "Aristotle's Distinction between *Energeia* and *Kinēsis*," in *Essays on Plato and Aristotle*, ed. J. L. Ackrill (Oxford: Clarendon Press, 1997); Sarah Waterlow, *Nature Change and Agency in Aristotle's Physics* (Oxford: Clarendon Press, 1982), pp. 183–186. Aristotle's opposition between motion and activity precludes actual perception being a motion. What I hope to show is that the requirements for perception as an activity extend to the processes occurring in sense organs. This fact, then, blocks Everson's contention that there is a κίνησις (alteration$_1$) in the eye, and an ἐνέργεια (alteration$_2$) in the faculty of vision supervening on it.

64. Richard Sorabji, "Body and Soul in Aristotle," in *Aristotle: De Anima in Focus*, ed. Michael Durrant (New York: Routledge, Inc., 1993), p. 172.

65. Richard Sorabji, "Intentionality and Physiological Processes: Aristotle's Theory of Sense Perception," in *Essays on Aristotle's De Anima*, ed. Martha C. Nussbaum and Amélie Oksenbury Rorty (Oxford: Clarendon Press, 1992), pp. 217–220.

66. Ibid., p. 217.

67. Thomas Aquinas, *Sentencia Libri De Anima*, Book II, Lecture 24, n. 551, in *Opera Omnia* iussu Leonis XIII P.M. edita. Cura et Studio Fratrem Predicatorum (Romae: Ex Typographia Polyglotta S.C. de Propoganda Fide, 1889). pp. 171–2.

68. Ibid., n. 552.

69. Ibid., n. 553.

70. Ibid., n. 555.

71. Ibid., n. 554.

72. Ibid.

73. Ibid., n. 557.

74. Everson, *Aristotle on Perception*, p. 88.

75. Ibid., pp. 88–89.

76. For a discussion of this chapter, which reaches similar conclusions by different means, see T. K. Johansen, *Aristotle on the Sense-Organs* (Cambridge: Cambridge University Press, 1998), pp. 274–280.

77. Kurt Pritzl, "On Sense and Sense Organ in Aristotle," *Proceedings of the American Catholic Philosophical Association* 59 (1985): p 261.

78. Everson, *Aristotle on Perception*, p. 139.

79. δοκεῖ δέ τισιν εἶναι ἀπορία καὶ περὶ τούτων· ἀδύνατον γάρ φασὶ τινες ἄλλον ἄλλῳ τὸ αὐτὸ ἀκούειν ἢ ὁρᾶν καὶ ὀσφραίνεσθαι· οὐ γὰρ οἷόν τ᾽ εἶναι πολλοὺς καὶ χωρὶς ὄντας ἀκούειν ἢ ὀσφραίνεσθαι· τὸ γὰρ ἓν χωρὶς ἂν αὐτὸ αὑτοῦ εἶναι. ἢ τοῦ μὲν κινήσαντος πρῶτον, οἷον τῆς κώδωνος ἢ λιβανωτοῦ ἢ πυρός, τοῦ αὐτοῦ καὶ ἑνὸς ἀριθμῷ αἰσθάνονται πάντες, τοῦ δὲ δὴ ἰδίου ἑτέρου ἀἀιθμῷ, εἴδει δὲ τοῦ αὐτοῦ, διὸ ἅμα πολλοὶ ὁρῶσι καὶ ὀσμῶνται καὶ ἀκούουσιν. ἔστι δ᾽ οὔτε σώματα ταῦτα, ἀλλὰ πάθος καὶ κίνησίς τις (οὐ γὰρ ἂν τοῦτο συνέβαινεν), οὔτ᾽ ἄνευ σώματος.

CHAPTER 5

The Difference between Αἴσθησις and Νοῦς

INTRODUCTION

Having examined the assumptions necessary for Aristotle's proofs that the intellect acts apart from the body, we can now evaluate the effectiveness of these proofs. It is clear that Aristotle wants to show that the intellect acts without the body and that it and the senses are alike in receiving form (without matter), becoming like and becoming identical with their respective objects. Moreover, it is also now clear that the activity of sensation is realized in physical organs without itself being an ordinary process of alteration. We can now summarize the general nature of perception and then draw some conclusions about the relation of the activity of the senses to their organs. Finally, we will be in a position to examine the differences between the senses and the intellect, which Aristotle cites in *DA* 3.4, and determine if these differences warrant his conclusion that νοῦς is separate, and what this separation amounts to.

THE NATURE OF PERCEPTION

In *DA* 2.5, after noting that perception is a case of being acted upon, Aristotle reaches his first conclusion that perception is a potency. The fact that the senses do not produce sensations of themselves, but that perception comes about only through the influence of external objects, shows that they are potencies in a unique way. "It is clear from this that the faculty of sensation has no actual but only potential existence" (417a7–8). Later in the chapter, he elaborates on the singular manner in which perception is a potency.

> Even the term "being acted upon" is not used in a single sense, but sometimes it means a kind of destruction by a thing's contrary, and sometimes rather a preservation of that which is potential by something actual which is like it, as potency is related to actuality. (417b2–5)[1]

Like other potencies, perception is a capacity for a certain kind of activity, and, in line with Aristotle's general principles, this capacity is defined in terms of its proper act. For example, the ability to see is defined in terms of the act of seeing, and this, in turn, is defined in terms of its proper object, color. More than being merely a capacity or ability for a certain type of activity, the potency of perception is characterized by the fact that the ability to perceive is not exhausted in being actualized. One's ability to see, for example, and to see the same thing, even when already engaged in an act of seeing, is never lost. The potency characteristic of perception, then, is essential to and distinctive of that activity. Thus, being essentially a potency defines the activity of perception. This means that the actualization of this potency is not of such a sort as to preclude actualization with respect to the same object. Hence, Aristotle says that the potency of perception is a preservation (σωτηρία) (417b4).

The fact that the essential potency of perception is preserved in its operation distinguishes it from ordinary processes involving a transition from potency to act, that is, alteration. In contrast to the actualization of perceptual potency, the actualization of a potency in ordinary alteration precludes any further alteration with respect to the same quality. Such cases of "being acted upon" are "a form of destruction of something by its contrary" (417b2–3) for not only is the previous quality destroyed, but even the ability to be acted upon in the same respect is eliminated insofar as it is destroyed. In ripening and changing from green to red, not only is the green color that an apple previously had lost or destroyed, but so is its ability to become red. Being red now, it no longer can *become* red. Clearly, then, the potency an organ has for perception differs from the potency a thing has for ordinary change. For this reason, Aristotle calls the process of perceiving an activity. Perception is either not an alteration or is one that should have its own name (417b6–7); it is an activity insofar as it corresponds to the exercise of knowledge (417b18–19).

As thus presented, a view of perception emerges with potency as essential to and characteristic of it and as thereby distinguished from ordinary alteration. That Aristotle intended to express this view of perception is confirmed by his claim that perception is the reception of form without matter. As wax receives the impression of a gold ring without the gold and not as gold, so the eye receives the color of an object without the object and not as the object. The manner in which a sense organ, for example, the eye, receives its proper sensible object, for example, color, is not as that quality exists in the object. The eye, therefore, does not become literally as red as the apple it sees. Instead, it takes on or receives the form red, both without matter and not as matter— that is, the eye comes to have the form red in a manner different from the way in which the apple has the form red. Furthermore, as the reception of form without matter is Aristotle's general principle for understanding all the senses, not just vision, so all the senses come to possess their objects in a nonliteral way.

Thus, perception is understood fundamentally in negative terms. Perception is the reception of proper sensibles (color, sound, etc.), or sensible form, *without* matter in the sense that what receives the form comes to have it in a *non*-matter-like way. Given the misleading and negative connotations of the terms "immaterial" and "spiritual" reception, it seems best to refer to this non-matter-like reception by the term "anahylic reception." Anahylic reception, then, characterizes both the senses and the intellect since they both become like their object and receive its form in a manner that is not like ordinary alterations. They each are anahylic receptions since each is *essentially* a potency, and the potency is not lost in being realized in either the actuality of perception or intellection. Just as the reception is understood negatively, so is its passivity. To the extent that the activity of perception comes about from an external object, Aristotle says that it is a kind of being acted upon, just as it is a kind of reception (418a1–3). Aristotle, however, says that perception is a non-passive (impassive) reception because it is not matter-like. Thus, he says both perception and thinking are impassive (429a15–18, 30–32).

Although perception is an activity, and immaterial in the sense that has been explained, it is still realized in material things. Aristotle is able to maintain that physical things (sense organs) can be the subjects of anahylic receptions since he believes that other purely physical processes are also activities. Such processes are in fact crucial to his explanation of senses and their organs. The change that the transparent medium undergoes as a result of the causal efficacy of light (and, by extension, also of color) is described as not being a motion and so is not an alteration. The effect of light and color is instead an activity, but one that is realized in unequivocally material things, that is, air and water. Because sight itself is an activity of receiving color, the medium for sight and the matter in which the perceptual ability is realized (i.e., the eye) must be composed of one of these two material substances that are capable of being the subject of the activity of color and light. Likewise, since all the senses require a medium, so all of them are activities realized in material things, that is, their organs. It is in fact this constraint that the material medium places on sense powers that allows one to draw further implications about the nature of senses and sense organs.

CONSEQUENCES AND LIMITATIONS OF PERCEPTION

The first constraint that the nature of perception places on each of its five species is the limitation of the range of each. Each sense is a potency for receiving one class of proper objects, one class of sense qualities. This limitation necessarily results from the fact that perception is an activity and an anahylic reception. If the physical process of perception were an ordinary alteration or a material reception, there would be no way that a given sense object could determine the physical constitution of the organ necessary for that object, since all types of material would be affected materially to the same extent. Yet, it is clear that Aristotle believes that the matter that is appropriate to a given sense organ is, in fact, necessitated by the function that the organ performs, that is, by the sense object the organ is ordered toward grasping. If perception were an ordinary case of alteration, this fact would block this necessitation since everything, not just sense organs, is materially affected by all of the tangible qualities (except pure elements, of course). Thus, if touch were a case of being affected in this way, everything would feel. Likewise, given that Aristotle believes that smells affect even non-perceptive things like air, if something is to smell, it must be able to be affected in a way unlike non-perceptive things (424b15–20). Presumably color and sound, too, affect everything materially. Thus, in order for there to be a kind of affectation by color and sound that is of a different sort than the manner in which everything is affected, the matter in which this sort of affection takes place must be of such a kind that it is affected in this different way. Thus, the organ for the perception of color must be made of a material that can be affected by color in a non-alterational (i.e., anahylic) manner as an activity. Since seeing and hearing are anahylic changes, they require some matter that can be affected anahylically. The eye, then, must be made of some matter that has the transparent, that is, water or air. Again, because the medium of hearing, air, receives sound anahylically, the organ of hearing, the ear, must be made of air. Thus, it is because perception is an anahylic reception of form that the proper object of sense constrains which matter can be suitable for which sense.

The fact that organs must be made out of matter that can be the subject of an anahylic reception at once allows the possibility of perception and limits the range of each organ. Since each organ needs to be made out of matter that is the subject of an appropriate activity and this sort of matter is the subject of just one activity, each sense is limited to that one sort of activity, the activity of receiving its objects anahylically. Although the eye must be made of something transparent in order to receive anahylically the activity of color, the transparent is receptive of *only* the activity of color. This entails, then, that the eye can only receive, that is, know, colors as its proper object. The same principle applies to each of the other senses. The medium of touch, which is in flesh, receives more than one set of contraries because it happens to be anahylically subject to them. It is nevertheless limited to these and no others. It is a consequence of the fact that the senses need to be made out of their appropriate matter, that they are restricted in the range of objects that they each may know. Given that the matter of each is in fact the subject of the activity of only one kind of sensible quality, and this is what constrains the sense to be made of this kind of material, each sense is restricted to knowing only this one kind of quality.

The next limitation imposed on perception by the fact that it is realized in organs is the limitation in the intensity of the objects it can receive, as shown by the fact that perceptual potency can be overwhelmed by intense sensibles. Aristotle explains the fact that sense powers are dazzled by claiming that each is the result of a mixture of material types that together constitute a "mean." The mean that is constitutive of each sense, then, allows each to be the subject of an activity (424a6–11). It is a consequence of this theory, however, that this mean can become upset by intense sensibles (424a29–34). When this occurs, the ability to perceive is lost. Thus, the fact that each organ must have a balance or mean of different material components in order to function entails that that balance can be lost and the sense power thereby overwhelmed. Taken generally, Aristotle's theory claims that whatever cognitive faculty is composed as a mean is subject to being overwhelmed. It is unclear why Aristotle believes that intense sensibles should upset the mean. Apparently, any matter that is the subject of an activity can receive only so much of that activity. The transparent, for example, can only receive light, and only to a limited degree of intensity.[2] Thus, given that each is a mean, Aristotle believes that sense organs set limits on the perceptual capacity, not only with respect to the range of objects that each sense can receive, but also on the intensity of those objects.

The final limitation to which the senses are subject concerns the content or objects of perception. For Aristotle, the objects of the senses are certain qualities of bodies that define the sense power of which they are the object. For instance, color is the quality possessed by bodies that animals are able to see, and so vision is defined in terms of color. However, color is more than that quality that an object possesses in virtue of which it is visible. Color, and all the sensible qualities, are said to belong to bodies independently of any capacity to produce perception (418a28–b2). Moreover, Aristotle believes that such qualities belong to bodies in virtue of the elements of which bodies are composed. Thus, because bodies are made of certain elements, they are endowed with certain corresponding properties that, in the presence of appropriate perceivers, produce the activity of sensation. Perceptual potency, then, is limited to being affected by objects having sensible qualities. Since an object has such qualities only in virtue of being material and composed of elements, perception can only be affected by what is so composed, and only in virtue of the material of which it is composed. It is not in virtue of every fact about an object that it can be perceived by one of the five senses, but only in virtue of the qualities belonging to bodies as bodies. The shape of an object, for instance, does not produce a perception of it, but one of the other sensible qualities does, and it is in virtue of these other sense qualities that shape is perceived. Thus, it is a consequence of Aristotle's account that perception of whatever is perceived comes about in virtue of the material of which the object is composed.

Each of these three limitations characteristic of perception results from the fact that perceptual potencies are realized in bodily, material organs. Each sense has only one class of objects because it is composed of matter subject to the anahylic activity of only that one class. The senses are dazzled because, as a mean of material components, an intensity of sensible objects upsets that mean. Finally, the senses are affected only by the qualities essential to bodies composed of elements. These three limitations of the senses indicate that they are necessarily bodily powers. They are also aspects that distinguish the senses from the mind. As will become clear, Aristotle believes that νοῦς has none of the limitations characteristic of the senses. From this fact, he concludes that νοῦς is a non-bodily power whose acts are not realized in any organ.

DE ANIMA 3.4 ON Aἴσθησις AND Νοῦς

At the beginning of *DA* 3.4, Aristotle declares his intention to delineate the features distinctive of νοῦς. "Concerning that part of the soul with which the soul knows and thinks (whether it is spatially separate, or only in its account), we have to consider what is its distinguishing characteristic, and how thinking comes about" (429a10–12). He is initially uncommitted concerning the question of the ontological status (i.e., the separation) of the faculty of thinking, for he apparently believes that such a question will be decided in the course of the ensuing discussion. So, rather than supposing that νοῦς is probably separate in a strong sense (which he does in other places of the *DA*) he leaves the question open.

The ontological question, however, is central to the project of delineating what is distinctive of νοῦς. At several points in the *DA*, Aristotle questions whether the mind is part of the sensitive faculty, being a kind of imagination. The sensitive faculty taken as a whole, that is, the αἰσθητικόν, includes all the particular sense faculties, even φαντασία, and is necessarily realized in bodily organs. If, however, νοῦς is not part of the sensitive faculty, it seems it would not be realized in any organ. While the chapter does present some discussion of the nature of the functioning of νοῦς, it does so by highlighting the fact that it is distinct from sensation. The distinctive characteristics of the mind's activity, then, give Aristotle the opportunity to draw the conclusion that it is ontologically distinct from the sense faculty, as well, and so is without any organ.

In addition to discovering what is distinctive of νοῦς, Aristotle also intends to show *how* thinking comes about. Moreover, it is clear that *DA* 3.5 provides his most detailed discussion of the mechanics of thinking, wherein he analyzes this activity in terms of his theoretical apparatus of act and potency. It is as a result of this analysis that he distinguishes the powers of the intellect as creative or active (ποιητικόν—430a12) and as potential (what becomes all things [πάντα γίνεσθαι—430a15]) or passive (παθητικὸς—430a24). Thus, it seems that Wedin is correct that the discussion of the intellect in *DA* 3.4 applies to the intellect as a whole. While Aristotle in Chapter 5 explains how thinking comes about, Chapter 4 is concerned primarily with discovering what is distinctive about the whole faculty of thought. The conclusions in Chapter 4 that νοῦς is separate or unmixed, then, are prior both textually and logically to the pronouncements in Chapter 5 that the mind, which makes all things, is "separate, impassive, unmixed" (430a18) and that it "alone is immortal and everlasting" (430a23). The conclusions reached in 3.4, then, are independent of any precision Aristotle will give them in 3.5.

Initially, Aristotle outlines the similarities between αἴσθησις and νοῦς in order to establish a basis of comparison from which he will conclude that the activity of the latter is not realized in the body.

> If thinking is like perceiving, it must be either a process of being acted upon by what is knowable, or something else of a similar kind. This part, then, must (although impassive) be receptive of the form of an object, and must be potentially such as its object, although not identical with it: as the sensitive is to the sensible, so must mind be to the knowable. (429a12–18)[3]

While he begins by making a conditional claim that they are similar, throughout this part of the chapter, and indeed the whole rest of the chapter, Aristotle assumes that they are similar. Indeed, Aristotle believes that νοῦς and αἴσθησις are similar on all these points, not only here, but also in other significant passages where he explains the nature of each. Here in *DA* 3.4, he says that νοῦς is a case of being acted upon, yet insofar as it is a cognitive faculty like αἴσθησις, it is not a strict case of this; neither thinking nor sensing is a case of alteration. Here, as he did for perception in *DA* 2.5, Aristotle claims that thinking is a case of being acted upon only in a loose sense. Similarly, mind, like sense, is at once impassive, in the sense just given, and is receptive of form. Mind, like sense, is also potentially like its object. In all of these points of similarity with αἴσθησις, Aristotle highlights features of νοῦς that, as we have seen, mark it as distinct from ordinary material processes, that is, alteration. νοῦς, like αἴσθησις, is an anahylic process, but as such it is not necessarily non-bodily since αἴσθησις is clearly a bodily process. Since both capacities are anahylic, however, differences between them according to those features characteristic of anahylic processes do distinguish αἴσθησις alone as realized in bodily organs and demonstrate that νοῦς is not so realized.

The Distinction According to Range of Objects

While the similarity between νοῦς and αἴσθησις inclined earlier thinkers toward the belief that they are two functions of the same faculty, Aristotle in his analysis tries to show that they are different. The first manner in which Aristotle says that νοῦς differs from αἴσθησις is according to their respective ranges. This difference, then, provides the basis on which to conclude that νοῦς is not realized in an organ. Having argued that both νοῦς and αἴσθησις are anahylic activities, Aristotle now shows that νοῦς is distinct by the fact that its range is unlimited.

It is necessary then, since mind thinks all things, that it should be "unmixed" (ἀμιγῆ), as Anaxagoras says, in order that it may be "in control," that is, that it may know; for anything appearing inwardly hinders and obstructs what is foreign. Hence the mind, too, can have no characteristic except its capacity to receive. (429a18–22)[4]

Aristotle asserts that νοῦς knows all things and apparently accepts the universality of its scope without argument. It is clear, however, that knowing all things means that νοῦς can receive the forms of all things. Given this universality, Aristotle believes this shows that mind is, in the words of Anaxagoras, unmixed (ἀμιγῆ). Aristotle thinks this conclusion is warranted because "anything appearing inwardly hinders and obstructs what is foreign." The argument runs thus:

What appears inwardly to a power hinders and blocks the reception of what is foreign.

Νοῦς knows all things, that is, no intellect is hindered in its reception.

Therefore, νοῦς is unmixed.

By saying that νοῦς is "unmixed," Aristotle means that the intellect is separate from the body in a strong sense. As a consequence, this argument of *DA* 3.4 depends on the assumption that cognitive powers that are not separate have a limited range of objects.

In order to successfully prove his conclusion, Aristotle needs to have a basis on which to relate the inwardly appearing (παρεμφαινόμενον) with being mixed. As we have seen, the fact that sensation requires a suitable material implies that each of the senses is limited to the reception of only one class of sensible object. Thus, if the senses are mixed (i.e., bodily) and they are hindered from receiving the forms of objects other than their proper objects, the link that inward appearance is supposed to provide between being mixed and being hindered should be found in the senses—that is, the principle "whatever has something appear inwardly is hindered and obstructed in receiving something foreign" generates the conclusion that "something which is not hindered is unmixed" *only if* "all mixed or bodily powers have something appearing inwardly that limits their range of receptivity." Unfortunately, Aristotle does not describe an organ's ability to sense in terms of lacking the inward appearance of something that would block the reception of its object, but such a description is implied by what he says about the material requirements for certain sense organs. "It is the colorless which is receptive of color, as the soundless is of sound. The transparent is colorless, and so is the visible or barely visible, such as the dark is held to be" (418b27–29). As has been shown, Aristotle attributes the suitability of organs for sensation to their having a material that is subject to an activity, but not subject to a material alteration. Here, he claims that it is the colorless and the soundless that are able to serve as the matter in which such activities are realized. The implication, then, is that having a color or sound would prevent each respective material from being able to receive either color or sound. Being colored or having color appear inwardly would prevent some matter from being the subject of the activity of anahylic reception of the forms of color. This is also confirmed when Aristotle asserts that "that which is to perceive white and black must be actually neither (and similarly with the other senses)" (424a8–11). It seems, then, that Aristotle makes a close connection between something undergoing anahylic reception and its lacking the form so received.[5] It remains to be seen whether it is necessary for his argument that he maintain this connection.

Thus, the nature of mind is such that it is completely cognitive in the sense that there is no limit to its receptivity. Since cognitively receptive things do not undergo material changes insofar as they are receptive (for a nature subject to such material changes prevents cognitive reception), so mind has a nature that is not subject to any material change whatsoever. This feature of νοῦς is in opposition to sense faculties (e.g., sight), which must be realized in some matter (e.g., water, which contains the transparent) that is of such a nature so as not to be susceptible to literal changes with respect to its object (e.g., coloration). Sense powers, however, are limited in their range insofar as their matter is subject to only one kind of anahylic reception, for example, the transparent only receives color. Sense organs are subject to literal and material alterations with respect to other sense qualities of which their matter is not the subject of anahylic reception. Eyes are affected by the tangible qualities: hard, dry and hot. The claim that mind knows all things means that it is materially affected by no sensible quality, and since every material thing is materially affected in some way, mind must not be realized in any material thing, as in an organ.

That this is probably Aristotle's intention is confirmed by what immediately follows this argument. The mind's only characteristic is its capacity to receive, for sense powers have other characteristics just to the extent that they are not receptive of certain qualities of objects.

That part of the soul, then, which we call mind (by mind I mean that part by which the soul thinks and forms judgements) is nothing actual until it thinks. So it is unreasonable to suppose that it is mixed with the body; for in that case it would become somehow qualitative, e.g., hot or cold, or would even have some organ, as the sensitive faculty has; but in fact it has none. It has been well said that the soul is the place of forms except that this does not apply to the soul as whole, but only in its thinking capacity, and the forms occupy it not actually but only potentially, (429a22–30)

Νοῦς has no actual existence until it thinks insofar as it is a cognitive faculty. The essential potency of cognition applies to it without restric-

tion, and its only actuality comes from its exercising its cognitive potency
in an act of knowing.

Thomas Russman, in *A Prospectus for the Triumph of Realism*, agrees
that Aristotle's first argument from *DA* 3.4 proceeds according to the
analogy with perception outlined above.[6] Russman argues, however, that
what we know about the nature of perception invalidates the assumptions that Aristotle makes about sensation, and so the conclusion that
the mind acts separately from the body is unwarranted. "(Aristotle)
claims to know the nature of 'body,' the nature of 'thought,' and that
the latter cannot be a property of the former. To arrive at this conclusion
he makes assumptions about the nature of body and the nature of
thought which seem highly questionable."[7] Russman believes that it is
an assumption of Aristotle's that "having a form in such a way as to *be*
something (of that form)" interferes with "having a form in such a way
as to know something (of that form)," an assumption that has been seen
to be false in the light of contemporary biology and neurophysiology.[8]
According to Russman, one can agree that seeing green, for instance,
does consist in receiving the form of green, but that this reception is
unimpeded by the fact that what receives it has a color of its own.

To receive the form of green necessary to see something green is only to be in
the sensory/neurological state that corresponds with seeing green. But if this is
all that is meant by "receiving the form of green," then already being a certain
color does not interfere with or distort it. The colors of the retina, optic nerve,
brain, and so on are, as such, irrelevant to what goes on when one sees a green
object. They do not distort the green color that one sees.[9]

Thus, Russman reasons, just as the pink retina can receive the form
of green without any hindrance or distortion, so a material intellect can
receive the forms of all material things without any hindrance or
distortion.

Aristotle has said that the intellect must have no material form whatever of its
own because this would interfere with reception of the forms needed for knowledge of all material things. He concludes that the intellect must operate independent of the body. But once we properly distinguish between the two ways of
"having form," illustrated by color perception, we see that the intellect might
very well have its own material form without this form distorting the forms by
which it knows. Operation independent of the body is therefore not required to

explain how the intellect can be open to the knowledge of all of nature. The Aristotelian argument for residual dualism is completely deflected.[10]

Since contemporary science has discredited the assumptions about sensation upon which Aristotle builds his argument in *DA* 3.4, his conclusion that the intellect is unmixed with, and separate from, the body does not follow.

Russman seems to have been unduly influenced by Aquinas in his reading of Aristotle's argument. Aquinas believes that Aristotle argues as follows: Since the intellect receives the forms of all bodies, it must lack the form of any body.[11] They seem to hold this interpretation despite the fact that Aristotle's text merely says that νοῦς knows all things (πάντα νοεῖ), not that it knows all bodies. Accordingly, Aquinas and Russman believe that the intellect exactly parallels the senses in the relation between receptivity and its own nature: Since the eye receives all colors, it must lack the form of any color.[12] Aristotle himself in texts other than *DA* 3.4 also seems to endorse this connection between receiving forms and not possessing them; the transparent receives color and the soundless sound.[13] It is not, however, necessary that this serve as a basis of his argument that νοῦς is separate from the body. The fact that he does not say that the intellect receives the forms of all bodies, but instead says that it knows all things, indicates that the analogy with the transparent is not what he bases his argument on.

Aristotle, in fact, makes two different claims with regard to the senses receiving the forms of their proper objects. On the one hand, as Aquinas and Russman have made apparent, he says that only matter that lacks a certain class of sensible object is capable of receiving such forms in sensation. For example, the transparent receives color and the soundless receives sound. On the other hand, only that which receives sensible form without matter is capable of sensing. For example, plants and other insensate things do not sense because they do not receive forms in this way, that is, anahylically.[14] The senses are thereby limited to one class of object—that is, what receives the form of color anahylically, not as an ordinary alteration, receives only such forms, but it is still subject to receiving other forms materially. It is only the second claim that is crucial to his argument, for only this second claim (and the sense power's implied limitation with regard to objects) generates the conclusion that νοῦς is non-bodily when coupled with the claim that νοῦς knows all things (as opposed to the claim that the intellect receives all bodily forms).

Thus, the discoveries of contemporary science about sense organs and the brain do not necessarily vitiate Aristotle's argument that the mind acts apart from the body. Aristotle can concede Russman's point that pink things (retinas) can receive the forms of colors. He can insist, however, that they do so only by receiving such forms anahylically, that is, as forms without matter and not as matter. He can also insist that receiving forms in this way entails that they receive only such form (i.e., the retina receives only the forms of colors). This being so, and because they are still bodily organs, Aristotle can insist that they are still subject to being affected by other forms (e.g., heat or hardness) in a material way. Thus, by claiming that νοῦς receives *all* forms, Aristotle is claiming that νοῦς is not at all affected materially, and so it is unmixed—that is, it is in no sense bodily, but separate in a strong sense. As long as retinas and other physiological apparatus of sensation still can be said to undergo anahylic reception of form (and nothing in Russman's argument suggests that they cannot), one is still led to the conclusion that the intellect is immaterial, given that it knows all things.

The Distinction According to Types of Impassivity

Another point of difference between the mind and the senses concerns their susceptibility to being dazzled. As νοῦς differs from αἴσθησις with regard to the range of objects each receives, so they differ according to the effect that intense objects have on their abilities to function.

But that the perceptive and thinking faculties are not alike in their impassivity is obvious if we consider the sense organ and sensation. For the sense faculty is not able to sense after an excessive sensible object; *e.g.*, of sound immediately after loud sounds, and neither seeing nor smelling is possible just after strong colours and scents; but when mind thinks the exceedingly knowable, it is not less able to think of slighter things, but even more able; for the faculty of sense is not apart from the body, whereas the mind is separate. (429a30–b6)[15]

Senses cannot sense after receiving intense sensible objects. Νοῦς, on the other hand, is able to think after thinking highly intelligible objects (νοήσῃ σφόδρα νοητόν) and, in fact, thinks better because of it. The reason, Aristotle says, is that αἰσθητικὸν is not apart from the body, while νοῦς is separate, which means separate enough in a strong sense that its activity is not realized in the body. Apparently, Aristotle reasons that the fact that αἴσθησις is realized in the body is the reason that perception can be overwhelmed by intense sensibles. He elaborates this connection when he says that the senses are a mean, and that this mean or balance becomes upset by intense sensibles (424a8–11; 424a29–34). From this analysis, one gathers that Aristotle assumes the general principle that whatever cognitive power is realized in the body is able to be dazzled by an intensity of its proper object. With this principle now explicit, one can summarize Aristotle's reasoning.

All bodily powers can be dazzled.

No intellect can be dazzled.

Therefore, no intellect is a bodily power.

This argument is primarily negative; it makes no claim about the nature of the intellect's objects. It merely points to the fact that the intellect is not dazzled as an indication that it is not a bodily power.[16]

Immediately after this conclusion, however, Aristotle does mention objects of the intellect as analogous to intense sensibles. Although the cogency of this argument does not depend on intense objects of the mind actually facilitating thinking, such objects help to confirm Aristotle's conclusion. One finds these intellectual objects of "greater intensity" in *Posterior Analytics* 1.2, where Aristotle describes the premises of a syllogism as more knowable than, and causing the knowledge of, the conclusion. While not described as excessive (σφόδρα), they are better known and are causative by being better known. "Hence if the primary premises are the cause of our knowledge and conviction, we know and are convinced of them also in a higher degree, since they cause our knowledge of all that follows from them" (72a31–33). If the conclusion is less clear than the premise, then it is more able to be known on account of the premises in the sense that the conclusion is knowable only when the premises are known. Clearly, when one considers the intensely intelligible, the analogy with the intensely sensible breaks down; an argument's premise is not "seen" in the way light is, and so it cannot overwhelm what "sees" it. This, however, is just Aristotle's point: light is seen because of a material organ, and thus that organ can be dazzled. The fact that premises do not have the same effect indicates that what "sees" premises, that is, νοῦς, does not have a material organ.

The Distinction According to the Materiality of Objects

The final argument of *DA* 3.4 is perhaps the most frustrating, for in it Aristotle seems the least committed, and least clear, as to how he draws his conclusion. Upon careful analysis, it seems that Aristotle argues for the distinction between νοῦς and αἴσθησις on the basis of the distinction between the content of each characterized quite generally.

> Since magnitude is not the same as what it is to be magnitude, nor water the same as what it is to be water (and so too in many other cases, but not in all, because in some cases there is no difference), one judges flesh and what it is to be flesh either by different faculties, or by the same faculty in different relations; for flesh is not found without its matter, but like "snub-nosed" it is a this in this. Now it is by the sensitive faculty that one judges hot and cold, and all qualities whose ratio constitutes flesh; but it is by a different faculty, either separate (χωριστῷ), or related to it in the same way as a bent line is related to itself when pulled out straight, that one judges what it is to be flesh. Again, among abstract objects "straight" is like "snub-nosed," for it is always combined with extension; but its essence (what it is to be what it was—τὸ δὲ τί ἦν εἶναι), if straight and what it is to be straight are not the same, is something different; let us call it duality. Therefore, we judge it by another faculty, or by the same faculty in a different relation. And speaking generally, as objects are separate for their matter so also are the corresponding faculties of the mind. (429b11–23)[17]

All that is clear from an initial reading of the passage is that the sense faculty knows the sensible qualities, and that at least two faculties (presumably sense and intellect) are employed either alone or together to judge sensible bodies like water and flesh, on the one hand, and what it is to be such things (i.e., their essences), on the other. Which faculty knows which object, however, is frustratingly obscure.[18]

Charles Kahn offers an interpretation of Aristotle's intention in this section of *DA* 3.4 according to which Aristotle is specifying which faculty, if any, νοῦς employs in its work of discrimination. According to Kahn, Aristotle is not interested in determining whether νοῦς is the faculty by which what it is to be flesh and what it is to be water are known or whether νοῦς is separate from the body. Aristotle is instead trying to determine whether νοῦς operates alone in judging flesh, without the sense faculty, or whether it uses the sense faculty in its work of making such judgments.[19] Kahn presupposes that Aristotle believes that νοῦς is what knows the essences of water and flesh, and so for him, the question really revolves around what knows these things (water and flesh) themselves. For Kahn, the answer is νοῦς plus the sense faculty.

Difficulties begin when we ask what contrast or contrasts Aristotle means to draw in regard to faculties. Clearly *nous* is the faculty which discerns the essences. But what faculty discerns the sensible bodies? Most (perhaps all) commentators seem inclined to suppose that it is by the sense-faculty that we apprehend water and flesh. But that is not what Aristotle says. He says that it is by sense that we discern hot and cold and other qualities that make up the matter of flesh; he does not say—and how could he say?—that it is sense which discerns the *logos* that is the form of flesh. In fact, it is not clear that this *logos* is distinct from the essence of flesh.[20]

According to Kahn, the sense faculty alone does not discern sensible bodies like flesh and water. The sense faculty alone can only discern sensible *qualities* like hot and cold. When these qualities are combined in a given proportion, that is, a *logos*, the sensible body results and νοῦς is required (either alone or in cooperation with sense) in order to know it. Since νοῦς judges "what it is to be flesh" and flesh is what it is due to the *logos* of its composition, νοῦς must be involved in judging even flesh.

Aristotle, then, is laying out two possible ways νοῦς operates in its knowledge of sensible bodies, according to Kahn:

The only interpretation that is both coherent with the context and compatible with Aristotle's general view is the following: since it is by *nous* that we discern the essence of flesh, then it is "by a different faculty (namely sense) or by the same faculty (i.e., *nous*) differently disposed" that we discern the matter-form compound of flesh (429b12–13). "For flesh is not without matter, but it is like the snub, this (form) in this (matter)." (429b14)[21]

Either we judge the material substances like water and flesh by νοῦς alone (but differently disposed) or we make such judgments by νοῦς plus a different faculty (sense). These two alternatives turn out not to be really opposed, but to be two ways of describing the one way νοῦς is employed in the discernment of sensible bodies.

So the question which Aristotle leaves open is whether we discern the concrete compound flesh by a different faculty, namely sense, or by *nous* "otherwise disposed," in its union with sense in perceptual judgement. And both alternatives are correct depending upon whether we take *aisthesis* narrowly, in which case it cannot perceive flesh as such but only the hot and the cold, or whether we take it broadly to include incidental sensibles in conjunction with *nous*. Now the second alternative is really equivalent to "*nous* otherwise disposed."[22]

Νοῦς operates separately if one considers sense to operate alone in its judgment of sense qualities. It must be said, however, that νοῦς is "differently disposed" if this is how one is looking at the situation. On the other hand, we judge bodies by another faculty in conjunction with νοῦς if we consider that the substances known are sensible bodies, and as sensible, the senses must be involved. Nevertheless, these are merely two ways of looking at the same cognitive process.

There are several reasons for resisting this reading of the text. First, Kahn's interpretation relies on a rather impoverished sense of αἴσθησις since, in his view, sense faculties only know proper sensibles. Because the senses can only know their own proper sensibles, that is, sensible qualities, they are unable to grasp the material things to which these qualities belong. Some use of νοῦς, either alone or with sense, is required to know sensible bodies. Aristotle, however, also uses αἰσθητικόν to refer to the sense faculty as a whole, which includes the central or common sense, and this seems to be the faculty that knows concrete particular things, not just their sensible qualities. Moreover, nonhuman animals have no share of νοῦς, but they are nevertheless able to sense particular sensible substances as substances. After all, the wolf also must be able to judge flesh, that is, what is a sheep and what is not, in order to eat, and to judge water in order to drink. There is no warrant, then, for Kahn's assumption that only some kind of employment of νοῦς would be able to judge water or flesh.

Another difficulty that one finds with Kahn's interpretation is that it requires that Aristotle be inconsistent in his reference to faculties. Aristotle's first use of "different" faculty and the "same faculty in a different relation" does not make it clear what the object of each is. "One judges flesh and what it is to be flesh either by different faculties, or by the same faculty in different relations" (429b12).[23] It is therefore plausible that they match up to objects in the way Kahn says they do: what it is to be flesh is judged by νοῦς, but flesh is judged by "a different faculty"

(in conjunction with νοῦς) or the "same faculty (νοῦς) in a different
relation." Aristotle's second use of "different faculty" refers to the one
that judges what it is to be flesh, and moreover, it may be separate
(χωριστῷ). "But it is by a different faculty, either separate, or related
to it in the same way as a bent line is related to itself when pulled out
straight, that one judges what it is to be flesh" (429b16–17).[24] This incongruity is reflected even in Kahn's own translation of the relevant
lines. "But one discerns the being-of-flesh by a different faculty [i.e.,
different from sense], either one that is (entirely) separate [from sense]
or by one related as a bent line is related to itself when straightened out"
(parentheses and brackets Kahn's).[25] Thus, what is "different" in the first
passage (1.12) is sense; it is different from what judges the essence of
flesh. In the second passage (1.16–17), what is different is νοῦς; it is
different from αἴσθησις, which judges hot and cold. Kahn, then, has
Aristotle saying first that a different faculty (in addition to νοῦς) judges
flesh, and later that a different faculty (from sense) judges the essence
of flesh, while first the same faculty (νοῦς) differently related judges
flesh and later a faculty (νοῦς) related to sense (as a bent line is related
to itself straightened) judges the essence of flesh. While this sort of shift
in reference may be required of Kahn's interpretation, there is nothing
in the text to suggest that Aristotle intended it. It seems, then, that the
text has to be twisted to fit Kahn's reading of it.

Furthermore, on Kahn's interpretation, there ends up being no distinction between objects or the faculties by which they are known. But
if this is the case, then Aristotle will not have succeeded in showing
anything beyond the assumptions that Kahn claims he starts with. For,
according to Kahn, Aristotle shows only that νοῦς knows both flesh and
what it is to be flesh (the *logos*) because knowing flesh really amounts
to knowing its essence, and so νοῦς by itself, or differently disposed by
acting in conjunction with sense, knows both. But it certainly seems
that, although he expresses it as a conditional, Aristotle believes that
flesh is in fact different from what it is to be flesh. The faculties that
know each, it seems, should not be the same. In addition, if it is true
both that νοῦς alone knows essences and that νοῦς in conjunction with
αἴσθησις knows flesh (which implies knowing its essence), then things
pertaining to the mind really are not as separate as their objects. Their
objects turn out to be the same, according to Kahn, and so νοῦς alone
and νοῦς with αἴσθησις turn out to be the same. If the passage shows

anything on Kahn's reading, it is only that sense does not really know sensible things (only sensible qualities) since νοῦς is the faculty responsible for such knowledge. This conclusion, however, is one of the unspoken assumptions Kahn believes Aristotle has in mind in saying that sense knows hot and cold and other sensible qualities. On Kahn's reading, then, the passage does not provide any new knowledge.

Although Kahn's interpretation does not seem to conform to the text, a positive account of the distinction between sense and intellect is still not readily apparent from this part of the *DA* 3.4. The first difficulty in providing such an account lies in determining how many faculties Aristotle is referring to. In order to decide that question, one must first decide how many kinds of objects he is giving examples of. First, he says that "we judge flesh and the essence of flesh either by different faculties or by the same faculty in different relations." He also says that we judge flesh by αἴσθησις and the essence of flesh by a faculty that is quite distinct (presumably from αἴσθησις) or related to it as a bent line is related to itself when pulled out straight. Finally, among abstract objects, we judge "straight" by one faculty, and "straightness" by another faculty or by the same faculty in a different relation. From these three cases, it seems that there are four kinds of objects about which we judge: flesh, the essence of flesh, the straight, and the essence of straight that is the same as duality. However, the essence of flesh and the straight are both somewhat abstract items, being mathematical. Like the ratio or proportion of the hot and cold that constitute flesh, the essence of flesh is a certain number realized in matter. In the same way, Aristotle says that the straight (as a property of geometrical figures) is always found with magnitude. Moreover, since apparently the same relation does or might obtain between the straight and the essence of straight as does obtain between flesh and the essence of flesh, it seems reasonable that the straight would include a necessary reference to matter, as the essence of flesh does. This is confirmed by the fact that Aristotle likens both flesh and the straight to the snub-nosed as having a necessary relation to matter. The four kinds of objects fit rather nicely into a three-tiered hierarchy of progressive abstraction: (1) the entirely material object of sense (flesh); (2) the somewhat abstract object that, nevertheless, has a necessary relation to matter (the essence of flesh and the straight); and (3) the most abstract objects (the essence of straight or duality). Aristotle seems to have had this ultimate in cognitive objects in mind when, at the beginning of the passage, he hints that there are some objects for which there is no difference between themselves and what it is to be themselves; there does not seem to be a difference between duality and what it is to be duality.

In order that the hierarchy of objects may illumine the nature of νοῦς, one must divine the import of the analogy that what judges flesh is related to that which judges the essence of flesh as a bent line is related to itself when pulled out straight. If it can be assumed, as seems reasonable, that we always and only judge flesh by αἴσθησις, then the question remains as to how we judge the essence of flesh. If the analogy with the bent line related to itself can provide a clue to his meaning, as it seems it must, then it appears that when we judge the essence of flesh, we do so by means of a faculty that is related to αἴσθησις as a bent line is related to itself when pulled out straight. In this analogy, the line is a common element on both sides of the relation; the difference is that on one side the line is bent, and so is the line in a different relation. This would seem to provide the key to understanding the cryptic phrase, "or the same faculty in a different relation." The faculty that judges the essence of flesh, then, is like the bent line in its relation to the αἰσθητ-ικον, which is like the line when pulled out straight. The faculty that judges the essence of flesh is either quite distinct from perception or is perception with something analogous to a bend in it. It is worth noting that the bend is not another substance added to the line, but rather is a form and so is in a sense immaterial. In the latter case, what judges the essence of flesh is αἴσθησις with something added, and since it is Aristotle's stated intention in 3.4 to find what is distinctive of νοῦς, it seems that νοῦς is that which is added.

The dizzying number of possibilities that result from Aristotle's various disjunctions injects a further element of confusion into an already confusing argument. The only sure element is that we judge flesh by αἴσθησις; the faculties by which we judge the other objects may be as many as three. On the one hand, sense (α) judges flesh, but another quite separate faculty (F_2) may judge the essence of flesh, while a third (F_3) faculty judges the straight, and yet another one (F_4) judges duality. Then again, it may be that α judges flesh, α in another relation (α^*) the essence of flesh, but F_3 still judges the straight and F_4 duality. On another hand, α may judge flesh, F_1 the essence of flesh, F_3 the straight, while F_3 in another relation (F_3^*) judges duality. If, however, there is reason to identify what judges the essence of flesh and what judges magnitude, as it seems there is, then the faculties form an orderly gradation: α judges flesh, α* judges the essence of flesh and magnitude, and another faculty, the addition of which to αἴσθησις puts it in another relation and allows for such judgments, judges duality.

Thus, if we judge the more abstract essence of straight (duality) by a faculty that is either separate from the faculty that judges the straight, or by that faculty in another relation, and straight is judged by αἴσθησις placed in another relation by the addition of νοῦς, then what judges the essence of straight is either completely separate or it is the faculty that judges both the essence of flesh and magnitude in another relation. Given that this faculty may itself be αἴσθησις in another relation, it is difficult to understand what Aristotle would mean by a faculty defined as {αἴσθησις-in-another-relation}-in-another-relation. Thus, the hierarchy of αἴσθησις, αἴσθησις bent into another relation by the addition of νοῦς and νοῦς as separate is certainly the simplest and most intelligible, given the confusion of Aristotle's text, and its very simplicity is the only thing that makes it more likely than its rivals. It seems most probable, then, that what judges duality is completely separate, what judges magnitude and the essence of flesh is the sense faculty differently related by the addition of something analogous to a form, and what judges flesh itself is the sense faculty. The conclusion that the faculty by which we judge the essence of straight is completely separate (if this is Aristotle's intent), then, depends on the prior argument that the faculty by which we judge the essence of flesh is either a separate faculty or the same faculty in a different relation. Fortunately, this argument is given in a modicum of detail and forms the core of this part of the chapter.

At the end of the day, it seems that Aristotle is simply none too committal in this, the third argument of *DA* 3.4, about the ontological status of νοῦς in relation to αἴσθησις. νοῦς alone may judge the essences of things, and it may be quite separate from αἴσθησις. On the other hand, it may be the case that that which is able to know the essence of flesh is αἴσθησις in another relation (which is like having a bend added to it), while αἴσθησις alone knows only flesh. If αἴσθησις is involved in the grasping of the essence of flesh, however, it is not able to do so in virtue of itself, but in virtue of being in another relation by the addition of something analogous to a bend. This something additional may still be worthy of being called separate in the strong sense, even though it involves αἴσθησις, if its activity is not realized in αἴσθησις and its organic nature. This accords with what Aristotle says elsewhere—that thought thinks its objects in images, which pertains to the αἰσθητικόν.[26] That which renders the αἰσθητικόν to be in a different relation, presumably νοῦς, would also count as being separate in a strong sense without being a separate substance. It is just the distinction in objects that shows that such a grasp is not so realized. Thus, while that by which we judge the essence of flesh may or may not be totally separate from matter, it is Aristotle's overall intention that what does grasp essences is separate just to the extent that its objects are. He does this on the basis that essences are not grasped by the sensitive faculty that grasps whatever it does in virtue of its organs.

The core argument, then, first establishes the connection between the ability of αἴσθησις to judge and the qualities of bodies. First, Aristotle asserts as an assumption that the objects of αἴσθησις are material. "Flesh cannot exist without matter." Further, he explains that flesh is constituted from the hot and the cold and other qualities, and we judge hot and cold and other qualities by αἴσθησις. More than listing mere facts about sense cognition, Aristotle is clarifying the connection between the objects of sense (proper sense qualities) and the fact that they belong to material things. Given that sense grasps material things and that material things are constituted by sense qualities, we judge flesh by αἴσθησις in virtue of sensible qualities proper to bodies—that is, in order that sense receive its proper objects, both sense and its objects must be realized in subjects composed of the elements. Since an object has the sensible qualities it does only in virtue of being material and composed of elements, the perceptual capacity can only be affected by what is so composed. Moreover, the sensitive faculty is affected by these elementally grounded qualities only in virtue of the materially constituted organ in which it is realized. For the eye is affected by color in virtue of having some matter, that is, water, that is subject to the anahylic activity of receiving form without matter, and all the senses are able to sense just insofar as their organs are appropriately composed (as a mean) of various elemental constituents (424a6–11). Thus, in order that the activity of perception take place, both the object perceived and the organ of the perceiving animal must be material objects composed of elements. Aristotle, then, seems to be making the quite strong claim that sensible qualities are perceived if and only if they are perceived by a sensitive

power that is realized in a material organ—that is, he seems to be claiming, for example, that if color is perceived, only an appropriately material
organ (i.e., the eye) can do so, and if an eye perceives something, then
its object is a material thing composed of elements.

With the connection between sensation and the qualities of bodies
thus established, the rest of the core argument draws what conclusion
it can from the difference between flesh and the essence of flesh. The
argument begins with the assumption, reasonable enough, that flesh is
other than the essence of flesh. It follows that if flesh is constituted by
the proper proportion of the sensible qualities, the essence of flesh is
not so constituted. Furthermore, αἴσθησις is the faculty that judges
flesh, and clearly there is a strong connection between αἴσθησις and
both what is required for its realization (a mean of the elements in its
organ) and its object (something having sensible qualities as a result of
its elemental composition). This premise may be taken to instantiate the
universal claim that if a cognitive power is essentially dependent on a
material organ, then its objects are elementally composed. What follows
from these premises is that if the essence of flesh is known, this does
not take place through a cognitive faculty that is materially realized, that
is, not by αἴσθησις. The argument, then, may be summarized as
follows:

No material things are its essence.

All material things are composed of elements.[27]

(Therefore, no essence is composed of elements.)

Every material cognitive power (sense) has objects composed of elements.

Therefore, the power that knows essences is not (entirely) a material power.

This argument, like the two that preceded it, is primarily a negative
one. All that the argument proves is that, because of differences between
itself and sense, mind is not realized in any material organ.

Given the confusing text of this argument, Aristotle expresses the
argument's conclusion with a certain amount of ambiguity. Either another faculty than sense judges the essence of flesh, or sense judges it by
being in another relation (having the addition of something like a bend).
What judges the essence does so precisely because it is either other than,
or an addition to, sense and thus does not do so by the action of sense

qualities. Therefore, either the faculty that judges the essence of flesh (1) is not constituted from the elements and so is separate (χωριστός), or (2) is αἴσθησις in another relation. Either way, it cannot be solely αἴσθησις as composed of the elements and in contact with something so composed that judges the essence of flesh. Thus, it is something either absolutely non-elemental (i.e., nonphysical) or it occurs through the addition of something differing from sense in being nonphysical. Aristotle generalizes his point by restating the conclusion in the claim that the physicality of a cognitive power corresponds to that of its objects. "And speaking generally, as objects are separable from their matter so also are the corresponding faculties of the mind" (429b11–23).

CONCLUSION

Having examined both Aristotle's understanding of perception and of its inherent limitations due to the fact that it is necessarily realized in material organs, one can understand the cogency of his reasoning in *DA* 3.4 that mind is separate from matter and the body. While the essential nature of perception as a potency indicates that it is not a case of ordinary alteration, nevertheless, it is still an essentially material activity. All sense powers require organs, and the organs must be of a definite and determinate material constitution, in order that they may receive sensible qualities of material things in an anahylic manner. For, were organs not so constituted, they would be subject only to the material alteration to which every other material thing is subject, and so would not serve their function of receiving form without matter and not as matter. Being material, then, is essential for sense organs to be able to grasp their objects. Being material, however, entails certain limitations characteristic of perception. Aristotle capitalizes on these limitations in his arguments in *DA* 3.4 for the separation of νοῦς. Each sense power is limited to receiving just one class of sense quality that its matter makes it fit to receive, while νοῦς is able to know, that is, receive, all things. This difference indicates that νοῦς is not material. Likewise, being material, every sense power is overwhelmed by intense sensibles, while νοῦς is never overwhelmed. This difference, too, indicates that νοῦς is not material. Finally, because there is an essential connection between being a mean of elemental components and perceiving sensible qualities, sense alone knows things composed of elements, while νοῦς knows essences that are not so composed. This difference, like those preceding it, indicates that νοῦς is not a material power.

In all of these arguments, Aristotle at once acknowledges certain similarities between the intellect and the senses, while noting that νοῦς is free from the limitations to which the senses are essentially subject on account of their organs. In order to see the cogency of his reasoning, however, it was first necessary to establish that the senses were essentially material despite the fact that they received form without matter. Prior to this, it was necessary to establish that νοῦς and the senses were similar in relevant respects, that is, that they both received form and did so anahylically, that they both became actually such as their object is from having only been potentially so, and that they both became one with their object. In order to see these similarities, however, it was necessary first to establish that Aristotle did have it in mind to prove that the intellect is separate in a strong sense, even though his commitment to hylomorphism prevented him from claiming that νοῦς is a separate substance. Despite apparent incongruities, obscurities and discontinuities of discussion, one can see that the doctrine of Aristotle throughout the *De Anima* enjoys remarkable consistency, subtlety and depth in its discussion of the nature of νοῦς as compared with the sense powers.

NOTES

1. οὐκ ἔστι δ᾽ἁπλοῦν οὐδὲ τὸ πάσχειν, ἀλλὰ τὸ μὲν φθορά τις ὑπὸ τοῦ ἐναντίου, τὸ δὲ σωτηρία μᾶλλον τοῦ δυνάμει ὄντος ὑπὸ τοῦ ἐντελεχείᾳ ὄντος καὶ ὁμοίου οὕτως ὡς δύναμις ἔχει πρὸς ἐντελέχειαν·

2. Cf. *Gen An* 5.1, 780a7–15.

3. εἰ δή ἐστι τὸ νοεῖν ὥσπερ τὸ αἰσθάνεσθαι, ἢ πάσχειν τι ἂν εἴη ὑπὸ τοῦ νοητοῦ ἢ τι τοιοῦτον ἕτερον. ἀπαθὲς ἄρα δεῖ εἶναι, δεκτικὸν δὲ τοῦ εἴδους καὶ δυνάμει τοιοῦτον ἀλλὰ μὴ τοῦτο, καὶ ὁμοίως ἔχειν, ὥσπερ τὸ αἰσθητικὸν πρὸς τὰ αἰσθητά, οὕτω τὸν νοῦν πρὸς τὰ νοητά.

4. ἀνάγκη ἄρα, ἐπεὶ πάντα νοεῖ, ἀμιγῆ εἶναι, ὥσπερ φησὶν Ἀναξαγόρας, ἵνα κρατῇ, τοῦτο δ᾽ἐστὶν ἵνα γνωρίζῃ· παρεμφαινόμενον γὰρ κωλύει τὸ ἀλλότριον καὶ ἀντιφράττει, ὥστε μηδ᾽αὐτοῦ εἶναι φύσιν μηδεμίαν ἀλλ᾽ἢ ταύτην, ὅτι δυνατόν.

5. Jonathan Barnes, "Aristotle's Concept of Mind," *Proceedings of the Aristotelian Society* 72 (1971–1972): 101–10. Barnes has essentially the same reading of the text as mine. Howard Robinson in "Aristotelian Dualism," in *Oxford Studies in Ancient Philosophy*, vol. 1 (Oxford: Oxford University Press, 1983),

pp. 123–44, also thinks that, for Aristotle, the limitless range of the intellect shows that it could not be a material power. "A faculty which had the capacity to receive forms from all the basic types of matter (and the intellect can certainly do that) would have itself not to possess matter, otherwise its range would be limited in just the sort of way the particular senses are limited" (p. 126). He goes on to explain that the forms that the intellect receives are of such heterogenous sorts that nothing material could receive all of them. "The combining of forms which could not be present together in the same matter shows that, in thought, they are not in matter at all" (ibid.).

6. Thomas Russman, *A Prospectus for the Triumph of Realism* (Macon, GA: Mercer University Press, 1987), pp. 24–25.

7. Ibid., p. 25.

8. Ibid., pp. 25–26.

9. Ibid., p. 26.

10. Ibid., pp. 26–27.

11. Thomas Aquinas, *Sentencia Libri De Anima*, Lib. III, lect. 7, n. 680 in *Opera Omnia* Iussu Leonis XIII P.M. edita. Cura et studio Fratrem Predicatorem (Romae: Ex Typographia Polyglotta S.C. de Propoganda Fide, 1889).

12. John F. X. Knasas in "Defense of a Thomistic Argument for Subsistent Soul," in *Aquinas on Mind and Intellect: New Essays*, ed. Jeremiah Hackett (Oakdale, NY: Dowling College Press, 1996), pp. 159–174, opposes Russman by also following Aquinas in the latter's belief that the colorlessness of the eye's pupil indicates that the eye receives color in a non-material way (pp. 163–167). Knasas, however, believes that the immaterial/spiritual reception occurs only in the form of the hylomorphic compound, which is the eye. He thus calls it the "reception of form by form" (p. 165). In order to maintain Aristotle's (and Aquinas's) contention that by the reception of intense sensibles (a contention instrumental in the next argument of *DA* 3.4), it seems best to maintain that some composite material substances can receive sensible forms in a non-standard material (anahylic) way. Thus, a given sense (power and organ together) is the subject of an immaterial activity only in a certain respect, that is, with respect to the proper object it receives. In this way the claim that mind is unmixed follows (more or less) directly from the claim that mind knows all things.

13. 418b27; 424a8–11.

14. *DA* 2.12, 424a32–b20.

15. ὅτι δ᾿οὐχ ὁμοία ἡ ἀπάθεια τοῦ αἰσθητικοῦ καὶ τοῦ νοητικοῦ, φανερὸν ἐπὶ τῶν αἰσθητηρίων καὶ τῆς αἰσθήσεως. ἡ μὲν γὰρ αἴσθησις οὐ δύναται αἰσθάνεσθαι ἐκ τοῦ σφόδρα αἰσθητοῦ, οἷον ψόφου ἐκ τῶν μεγάλων ψόφων, οὐδ᾿ἐκ τῶν ἰσχυρῶν χρωμάτων καὶ ὀσμῶν οὔτε ὁρᾶν οὔτε ὀσμᾶσθαι· ἀλλ᾿ὁ νοῦς ὅταν τι νοήσῃ σφόδρα νοητόν, οὐχ ἧττον νοεῖ τὰ ὑποδεέστερα, ἀλλὰ καὶ μᾶλλον· τὸ μὲν γὰρ αἰσθητικὸν οὐκ ἄνευ σώματος, ὁ δὲ χωριστός.

16. See Johnathan Lear, *Aristotle and the Desire to Understand* (Cambridge: Cambridge University Press, 1988), pp. 114–115.

17. Ἔπει δ᾿ἄλλο ἐστὶ τὸ μέγεθος καὶ τὸ μεγέθει εἶναι καὶ ὕδωρ καὶ ὕδατι εἶναι (οὕτω δὲ καὶ ἐφ᾿ἑτέρων πολλῶν, ἀλλ᾿οὐκ ἐπὶ πάντων· ἐπ᾿ἐνίων γὰρ τούτόν ἐστι), τὸ σαρκὶ εἶναι καὶ σάρκα ἢ ἄλλῳ ἢ ἄλλως ἔχοντι κρίνει· ἡ γὰρ σὰρξ οὐκ ἄνευ τῆς ὕλης, ἀλλ᾿ὥσπερ τὸ σιμὸν, τόδε ἐν τῷδε. τῷ μὲν οὖν αἰσθητικῷ τὸ θερμὸν καὶ τὸ ψυχρὸν κρίνει, καὶ ὧν λόγος τις ἡ σάρξ· ἄλλῳ δὲ, ἤτοι χωριστῷ ἢ ὡς ἡ κεκλασμένη ἔχει πρὸς αὐτὴν ὅταν ἐκταθῇ, τὸ σαρκὶ εἶναι κρίνει. πάλιν δ᾿ ἐπί τῶν ἐν ἀφαιρέσει ὄντων τὸ εὐθύ ὡς τὸ σιμόν· μετὰ συνεχοῦς γὰρ· τὸ δὲ τί ἦν εἶναι, εἰ ἔστιν ἕτερον τὸ εὐθεῖ εἶναι καὶ τὸ εὐθύ, ἄλλο· ἔστω γὰρ δυάς. ἑτέρῳ ἄρα ἢ ἑτέρως ἔχοντι κρίνει. ὅλως ἄρα ὡς χωριστὰ τὰ πράγματα τῆς ὕλης, οὕτω καὶ τα περὶ τὸν νοῦν.

18. Few commentators offer much help in understanding the passage. W. D. Ross, ed. *Aristotle De Anima* (Oxford: Clarendon Press, 1961), text and commentary, for instance, says only that "it is difficult to see in what sense reason can be thought of as bent and sense-perception as straight, or *vice versa*; it seems probable that A. is merely saying that . . . (they) are either separate faculties or one faculty operating on different objects" (p. 293).

19. Kahn, "Aristotle on Thinking," p. 370. For a similar interpretation, see also Malcolm Lowe, "Aristotle on Kinds of Thinking," in *Aristotle's De Anima in Focus*, ed. Michael Durrant (New York: Routledge, Inc., 1993), pp. 110–127.

20. Kahn, "Aristotle on Thinking," p. 370.

21. Ibid.

22. Ibid., p. 371.

23. τὸ σαρκὶ εἶναι καὶ σάρκα ἢ ἄλλῳ ἢ ἄλλως ἔχοντι κρίνει.

24. ἄλλῳ δὲ, ἤτοι χωριστῷ ἢ ὡς ἡ κεκλασμένη ἔχει πρὸς αὐτὴν ὅταν ἐκταθῇ, τὸ σαρκὶ εἶναι κρίνει.

25. Kahn, "Aristotle on Thinking," p. 370.

26. 431b3; see also 432b9 and 445b16.

27. Actually, it is almost certainly true that Aristotle would accept both this claim and the claim that *only* material things are composed of elements. Technically, this additional claim is required for the argument's validity.

Bibliography

Abel, Donald C. "Intellectual Substance as Form of the Body in Aquinas." *American Catholic Philosophical Quarterly* 69, supplement (1995): 227–236.

Ackrill, J. L. "Aristotle's Distinction between *Energeia* and *Kinēsis*." In *Essays on Plato and Aristotle*, edited by J. L. Ackrill. Oxford: Clarendon Press, 1997.

Annas, Julia. "Aristotle on Memory and the Self." In *Essays on Aristotle's* De Anima, edited by Martha C. Nussbaum and Amélie Oksenberg Rorty, 297–312. Oxford: Clarendon Press, 1992.

Aquinas, Thomas. *Aristotle's* De Anima *in the Version of William of Moerbeke and the Commentary of St. Thomas Aquinas.* Translated by Kenneth Foster and Sylvester Humphries. New Haven and London: Yale University Press, 1951.

———. *Basic Writings of Saint Thomas Aquinas.* Edited by Anton C. Pegis. New York: Random House, 1945.

———. *Opera Omnia.* Iussu Leonis XIII P. M. edita. Cura et studio Fratrum Predicatorum. Romae: Ex Typographia Polyglotta S. C. de Propoganda Fide, 1889.

———. *Quaestiones Disputatae.* Edited by P. Mandonnet. Paris: Lethielleux, 1925.

———. *Quaestiones Disputatae.* Edited by P. Caramello. Taurini: Marietti, 1965.

———. *Summa Theologiae.* Edited by Petrus Caramello. Taurini: Marietti, 1952.

Aristotle. *Aristote De l'âme.* Edited by A. Jannone and E. Barbotin. Paris: Budé, 1966. Text and French translation.

———. *Aristotelis opera omnia, Graece et Latine.* Edited by U. C. Bussemaker, J. F. Dübner, and E. Heitz. Paris: A. F. Didot, 1848–1874.

————. *Aristotle De Anima.* Translated by R. D. Hicks. Cambridge: Cambridge University Press, 1907. Introduction and notes.

————. *Aristotle De Anima.* Edited by W. D. Ross. Oxford: Clarendon Press, 1961. Text and commentary.

————. *Aristotle: De Anima (On the Soul).* Translated by Hugh Lawson-Tancred. New York: Penguin, 1986. With an introduction and notes.

————. *Aristotle on Coming to Be and Passing Away.* Edited by Harold H. Joachim. Oxford Classical Text. Oxford: Clarendon Press, 1922.

————. *Aristotle: Posterior Analytics.* Translated by Hugh Tredennick. Loeb Classical Library. Cambridge: Harvard University Press, 1984.

————. *Aristotle's De Anima. Books II and III.* Translated by D. W. Hamlyn. Oxford: Clarendon Press, 1968. Translation and commentary.

————. *Aristotle's De Motu Animalium.* Edited by Martha C. Nussbaum. Princeton: Princeton University Press, 1978. Text, translation and commentary.

————. *Aristotle's Metaphysics.* Edited by W. D. Ross. Oxford Classical Text. Oxford: Clarendon Press, 1924.

————. *De Anima.* In *The Basic Works of Aristotle,* edited by Richard McKeon. Translated by J. A. Smith. New York: Random House, 1941.

————. *De Anima.* Edited by W. D. Ross. Oxford Classical Text. Oxford: Clarendon Press, 1956.

————. *De Generatione Animalium.* In *The Basic Works of Aristotle,* edited by Richard McKeon Translated by Arthur Platt. New York: Random House, 1941.

————. *De Generatione Animalium.* Edited by H. J. Drossaart Lulofs. Oxford Classical Text. Oxford: Clarendon Press, 1965.

————. *De la Génération et de la Corruption.* Edited by Charles Mugler. Paris: Budé, 1966.

————. *Metaphysica.* Edited by W. Jaeger. Oxford Classical Text. Oxford: Clarendon Press, 1957.

————. *On the Soul.* Translated by W. S. Hett. Loeb Classical Library. Cambridge, MA: Harvard University Press, 1986.

————. *Physica.* Edited by W. D. Ross. Oxford Classical Text. Oxford: Clarendon Press, 1950.

————. *Physique.* Edited by Henri Carteron. Paris: Budé, 1969.

Barnes, Jonathan. "Aristotle's Concept of Mind," Proceedings of the Aristotelian Society 72 (1971–1972): 101–110.

Block, Ned. "What Is Functionalism?" In *Readings in Philosophy of Psychology,* edited by Ned Block, 171–184. Cambridge, MA: Harvard University Press, 1980.

Boyd, Richard. "Materialism without Reductionism: What Physicalism Does Not Entail." In *Readings in Philosophy of Psychology,* edited by Ned Block, 67–106. Cambridge, MA: Harvard University Press, 1980.

Brennan, Sheila O'Flynn. "Sensing and the Sensitive Mean in Aristotle." *New Scholasticism* 47 (1973): 270–310.

Burnyeat, M. F. "Is an Aristotelian Philosophy of Mind Still Credible? A Draft." In *Essays on Aristotle's* De Anima, edited by Martha C. Nussbaum and Amélie Oksenberg Rorty, 15–26. Oxford: Clarendon Press, 1992.

Bynum, Terrell Ward. "A New Look at Aristotle's Theory of Perception." In *Aristotle*: De Anima *in Focus*, edited by Michael Durrant, 90–109. New York: Routledge, Inc., 1993.

Casey, Gerard. "Minds and Machines." *American Catholic Philosophical Quarterly* 66 (1992): 57–80.

Churchland, Paul M. *Matter and Consciousness*. Cambridge, MA: MIT Press, 1984.

Cohen, S. Marc. "Hylomorphism and Functionalism." In *Essays on Aristotle's* De Anima, edited by Martha C. Nussbaum and Amélie Oksenberg Rorty, 57–74. Oxford: Clarendon Press, 1992.

———. "Sensations, Colors, and Capabilities in Aristotle." *New Scholasticism* 52 (1978): 558–568.

———. "St. Thomas Aquinas on the Immaterial Reception of Sensible Forms." *The Philosophical Review* 91, no. 2 (1982): 193–209.

Coulter, Gregory J. "Mental and Bodily Relations: Is There a Mind-body Problem?" *American Catholic Philosophical Quarterly* 66, supplement (1992): 251–265.

Davidson, Donald. "Mental Events." In *Essays on Actions and Events*, edited by Donald Davidson 207–224. Oxford: Oxford University Press, 1980.

Decaen, Christopher. "Elemental Virtual Presence in St. Thomas." *The Thomist* 64 (2000): 271–300.

———. "The Viability of Aristotelian-Thomistic Color Realism." *The Thomist* 65 (2001): 179–222.

Descartes, René. *Meditations Concerning First Philosophy*. Translated by Laurence J. Lafleur. Indianapolis: Bobbs-Merrill Co., Inc., 1960.

———. *The Philosophical Works of Descartes*. Edited and translated by E. S. Haldane and G.R.T. Ross. 2 vols. Cambridge: Cambridge University Press, 1967.

Everson, Stephen. *Aristotle on Perception*. Oxford: Clarendon Press, 1997.

Foster, David Ruel. "Aquinas' Arguments for Spirit." *American Catholic Philosophical Quarterly* 65, supplement (1991).

———. "Aquinas on the Immateriality of the Intellect." *The Thomist* 55, no. 3 (1991).

Franks, Joan. "*Nous* as Human Form: Reflections on the *De Anima*." *American Catholic Philosophical Quarterly* 69, supplement (1995): 249–257.

Frede, Michael. "On Aristotle's Conception of the Soul." In *Essays on Aristotle's*

De Anima, edited by Martha C. Nussbaum and Amélie Oksenberg Rorty, 93–108. Oxford: Clarendon Press, 1992.

Freeland, Cynthia. "Aristotle on the Sense of Touch." In *Essays on Aristotle's* De Anima, edited by Martha C. Nussbaum and Amélie Oksenberg Rorty, 227–248. Oxford: Clarendon Press, 1992.

Geach, Peter. *God and the Soul*. London: Routledge and Kegan Paul, 1969.

Granger, Herbert. "Aristotle and the Functionalist Debate." *Aperion* 23, no. 1 (1990).

Haldane, John J. "Aquinas on Sense Perception." *The Philosophical Review* 92, no. 2 (1983): 233–239.

Heinaman, Robert. "Aristotle and the Mind-body Problem." *Phronesis* 35, no. 1 (1990).

Hutchinson, D. S. "Restoring the Order of Aristotle's *De Anima*." *Classical Quarterly* 37, no. 2 (1987).

Johansen, T. K. *Aristotle on the Sense-Organs*. Cambridge: Cambridge University Press, 1998.

Kahn, Charles H. "Aristotle on Thinking." In *Essays on Aristotle's* De Anima, edited by Martha C. Nussbaum and Amélie Oksenberg Rorty, 359–380. Oxford: Clarendon Press, 1992.

Kenny, Anthony. *Aquinas on Mind*. London: Routledge, 1993.

————. "Intellect and Imagination in Aquinas." In *Aquinas: A Collection of Critical Essays*, edited by Anthony Kenny, 273–296. Notre Dame, IN: University of Notre Dame Press, 1976.

Kim, Jaegwon. *Philosophy of Mind*. Boulder, CO: Westview Press, 1996.

Knasas, John F. X. "Defense of a Thomistic Argument for Subsistent Soul." In *Aquinas on Mind and Intellect: New Essays*, edited by Jeremiah Hackett, 159–174. Oakdale, NY: Dowling College Press, 1996.

Kosman, L. A. "What Does the Maker Mind Make?" In *Essays on Aristotle's* De Anima, edited by Martha C. Nussbaum and Amélie Oksenberg Rorty, 343–358. Oxford: Clarendon Press, 1992.

Koterski, Joseph W. "Recognizing One of Aquinas' Debts to Neoplatonism." In *Aquinas on Mind and Intellect: New Essays*, edited by Jeremiah Hackett, 5–14. Oakdale, NY: Dowling College Press, 1996.

Kretzmann, Norman. "Philosophy of Mind." In *The Cambridge Companion to Aquinas*, edited by Norman Kretzmann and Eleonore Stump, 128–159. Cambridge: Cambridge University Press, 1993.

Lear, Jonathan. *Aristotle: The Desire to Understand*. Cambridge: Cambridge University Press, 1988.

Lloyd, G.E.R. "Aspects of the Relation between Aristotle's Psychology and His Zoology." In *Essays on Aristotle's* De Anima, edited by Martha C. Nussbaum and Amélie Oksenberg Rorty, 147–168. Oxford: Clarendon Press, 1992.

Lowe, Malcolm F. "Aristotle on Kinds of Thinking." In *Aristotle: De Anima in Focus*, edited by Michael Durrant, 110–127. New York: Routledge, Inc., 1993.

Lycan, William G. "Functionalism (1)." In *A Companion to the Philosophy of Mind*, edited by Samuel Guttenplan, 317–322. Oxford: Blackwell Publishers, 1994.

Martin, James T. H. "Sense and Intentionality: Aristotle and Aquinas." In *Aquinas on Mind and Intellect: New Essays*, edited by Jeremiah Hackett, 175–184. Oakdale, NY: Dowling College Press, 1996.

Matthews, Gareth B. "*De Anima* 2.2–4 and the Meaning of *Life*." In *Essays on Aristotle's* De Anima, edited by Martha C. Nussbaum and Amélie Oksenberg Rorty, 185–194. Oxford: Clarendon Press, 1992.

McCabe, Herbert. "The Immortality of the Soul." In *Aquinas: A Collection of Critical Essays*, edited by Anthony Kenny, 297–306. Notre Dame, IN: University of Notre Dame Press, 1976.

Mensch, James R. "Aristotle and the Overcoming of the Subject-object Dichotomy." *American Catholic Philosophical Quarterly* 65 (1991): 465–482.

———. "The Mind-body Problem: Phenomenological Reflections on an Ancient Solution." *American Catholic Philosophical Quarterly* 68 (1994): 30–56.

Modrak, Deborah. "Aristotle, the First Cognitivist." *Apeiron* 23, no. 1 (1990).

———. *Aristotle. The Power of Perception*. Chicago: University of Chicago Press, 1987.

———. "The *Nous*-body Problem in Aristotle." *Review of Metaphysics* 44, no. 4 (1990–1999): 755–774.

Murnion, William E. "Aquinas's Earliest Philosophy of Mind: "Mens" in the *Commentary on the Sentences* and the Contemporaneous Writings." In *Aquinas on Mind and the Intellect: New Essays*, edited by Jeremiah Hackett, 45–84. Oakdale, NY: Dowling College Press, 1996.

Nelson, John O. "Was Aristotle a Functionalist?" *Review of Metaphysics* 43, no. 4 (1989–1990).

Nussbaum, Martha C., and Hilary Putnam. "Changing Aristotle's Mind." In *Essays on Aristotle's* De Anima, edited by Martha C. Nussbaum and Amélie Oksenberg Rorty, 27–56. Oxford: Clarendon Press, 1992.

Olshewski, Thomas. "Functionalism, Old and New." *History of Philosophy Quarterly* 9, no. 3 (1992).

Osborne, Catherine. "Aristotle's *De Anima* 3, 2: How Do We Perceive That We See and Hear?" *Classical Quarterly* 33, no. 2 (1983).

Owens, Joseph. "Form and Cognition in Aristotle." *Ancient Philosophy* 1 (1980): 17–28.

Pritzl, Kurt. "On Sense and Sense Organ in Aristotle." *Proceedings of the American Catholic Philosophical Association* 59 (1985): 258–274.

Putnam, Hilary. "Brains and Behavior." In *Readings in Philosophy of Psychology*, edited by Ned Block, 24–36. Cambridge, MA: Harvard University Press, 1980.

———. "Philosophy and Our Mental Life." In *Readings in Philosophy of Psychology*, edited by Ned Block, 134–143. Cambridge, MA: Harvard University Press, 1980.

———. "Why Functionalism Didn't Work." In *Words and Life*, edited by James Conant. Cambridge, MA: Harvard University Press, 1994.

Robinson, Howard. "Aristotelian Dualism." In *Oxford Studies in Ancient Philosophy*, edited by Julia Annas. Vol. 1, pp. 123–144. Oxford: Oxford University Press, 1983.

———. "Form and the Immateriality of the Intellect from Aristotle to Aquinas." In *Oxford Studies in Ancient Philosophy*, Henry Blumenthal and Howard Robinson. supp. vol. (1991): 207–226.

———. "Mind and Body in Aristotle." *Classical Quarterly* 28 (1978): 105–124.

Romeyer-Dherbey, Gilbert. "Voir et Toucher: Le Problème de la Preeminence d'un Sens chez Aristote." *Revue metaphysique et morale* 96 (1991): 437–454.

Rorty, Amélie Oksenberg. "*De Anima* and Its Recent Interpreters." In *Essays on Aristotle's De Anima*, edited by Martha C. Nussbaum and Amélie Oksenberg Rorty, 7–14. Oxford: Clarendon Press, 1992.

Russman, Thomas A. *A Prospectus for the Triumph of Realism*. Macon, GA: Mercer University Press, 1987.

Schofield, Malcolm. "Aristotle on the Imagination." In *Essays on Aristotle's De Anima*, edited by Martha C. Nussbaum and Amélie Oksenberg Rorty, 249–278. Oxford: Clarendon Press, 1992.

Sheehan, Peter. "Aquinas on Intentionality." In *Aquinas: A Collection of Critical Essays*, edited by Anthony Kenny, 307–321. Notre Dame, IN: University of Notre Dame Press, 1976.

Shields, Christopher. "Soul as Subject in Aristotle's *De Anima*." In *Essays in Ancient Greek Philosophy*, edited by Anthony Preus and John P. Anton. Albany, NY: State University of New York Press, 1992.

Silverman, Allan. "Color and Color-perception in Aristotle's *De Anima*." *Ancient Philosophy* 9, no. 2 (1989): 271–292.

Sisko, John. "Material Alteration and Cognitive Activity in Aristotle's *De Anima*." *Phronesis* 41, no. 2 (1996).

Slakey, Thomas J. "Aristotle on Sense Perception." In *Aristotle: De Anima in Focus*, edited by Michael Durrant, 75–89. New York: Routledge, Inc., 1993.

Sorabji, Richard. "Body and Soul in Aristotle." In *Aristotle: De Anima in Focus*, edited by Michael Durrant, 162–196. New York: Routledge, Inc., 1993.

———. "From Aristotle to Brentano: The Development of the Concept of Intentionality." In *Festschrift for A. C. Lloyd: On the Aristotelian Tradition,* edited by H. Blumenthal and H. Robinson. *Oxford Studies in Ancient Philosophy,* supp. vol. Oxford: Oxford University Press, 1991.

———. "Intentionality and Physiological Processes: Aristotle's Theory of Sense Perception." In *Essays on Aristotle's* De Anima, edited by Martha C. Nussbaum and Amélie Oksenberg Rorty, 195–227. Oxford: Clarendon Press, 1992.

South, James B. "Intellectual Knowledge of Material Particulars in Thomas Aquinas: An Introduction." In *Aquinas on Mind and the Intellect: New Essays,* edited by Jeremiah Hackett, 85–116. Oakdale, NY: Dowling College Press, 1996.

Sweeney, Michael J. "Thomas Aquinas on Intellect, Infinity and Immateriality." In *Aquinas on Mind and Intellect: New Essays,* edited by Jeremiah Hackett, 117–158. Oakdale, NY: Dowling College Press, 1996.

Ward, Julie K. "Souls and Figures: Defining the Soul in *De Anima* II, 3." *Ancient Philosophy* 16 (1996).

Waterlow, Sarah. *Nature Change and Agency in Aristotle's* Physics. Oxford: Clarendon Press, 1982.

Wedin, Michael V. "Aristotle and the Mechanics of Thought." *Ancient Philosophy* 9, no. 1 (1989). History of Philosophy Quarterly.

———. "Keeping the Matter in Mind, Aristotle on the Passions and the Soul." *Pacific Philosophical Quarterly* 76, nos. 3–4 (1995).

———. *Mind and Imagination in Aristotle.* New Haven: Yale University Press, 1988.

———. "Tracking Aristotle's Νοῦς." In *Aristotle: De Anima in Focus,* edited by Michael Durrant, 128–161. New York: Routledge, Inc., 1993.

Whiting, Jennifer. "Living Bodies." In *Essays on Aristotle's* De Anima, edited by Martha C. Nussbaum and Amélie Oksenberg Rorty, 75–92. Oxford: Clarendon Press, 1992.

Wilkes, K. V. *Physialism.* Atlantic Highlands, NJ: Humantities Press, 1978.

———. "*Psuchē* versus the Mind." In *Essays on Aristotle's* De Anima, edited by Martha C. Nussbaum and Amélie Oksenberg Rorty, 109–128. Oxford: Clarendon Press, 1992.

Witt, Charlotte. "Dialectic, Motion and Perception: *De Anima,* Book 1." In *Essays on Aristotle's* De Anima, edited by Martha C. Nussbaum and Amélie Oksenberg Rorty, 169–184. Oxford: Clarendon Press, 1992.

Index

About the Author

JOSEPH M. MAGEE is Director of Campus Ministry at the Catholic Student Center, Sam Houston State University.